THE
GOLDEN THREAD
OF ONENESS

A.R.E. MEMBERSHIP SERIES

THE GOLDEN THREAD OF ONENESS
A JOURNEY INWARD TO THE
UNIVERSAL CONSCIOUSNESS

by Jon Robertson
and the
Editors of the A.R.E.

A.R.E. Press • Virginia Beach • Virginia

A.R.E. Press
Sixty-Eighth & Atlantic Avenue
P.O. Box 656
Virginia Beach, VA 23451-0656

Robertson, Jon.
    The golden thread of oneness : a journey inward to the univer-
sal consciousness / by Jon Robertson and the editors of the A.R.E.
        p.   cm.—(A.R.E. membership series : 5)
    Includes bibliographical references.
    ISBN 0-87604-392-9
    1. Association for Research and Enlightenment. 2. Mysticism.
3. Spiritual life. I. Title. II. Series.
BP605.A77R63   1997
299'.93—dc21   97-16705

The *A.R.E. Membership Series*

This book, *The Golden Thread of Oneness: A Journey Inward to the Universal Consciousness,* is another in a continuing series of books that is published by the Association for Research and Enlightenment, Inc., for individuals who are especially interested in their personal and spiritual growth and transformation.

The A.R.E. was founded in 1931 as a nonprofit organization to study, research, and disseminate information on ESP, dreams, holistic health, meditation, and life after death. The A.R.E. continues its mission today, nurturing a worldwide membership with conferences, study groups, and a variety of publications—all aimed at helping seekers find paths that will lead to a more fulfilling life, mentally, physically, and spiritually. The hallmark of A.R.E.'s publications is to be helpful and hopeful. A.R.E. is committed to assisting in personal growth and making available nourishing entertainment.

Many of the books published by A.R.E. are available in bookstores throughout the world and all are available directly from the A.R.E.'s mail-order catalogs.

Three new books in this *A.R.E. Membership Series* are sent at no cost each year to individuals who are Sponsoring members or Life members of A.R.E. Each of the titles in this series will become available, in the year after initial publication, for purchase by individuals throughout the world who are interested in individual growth and transformation.

For more information about membership benefits of the nonprofit Association for Research and Enlightenment, Inc., please turn to the last page in this volume.

The A.R.E. Membership Series:

Contents

PREFACE

AN EXPERIENCE OF THE HEART

The human heart has ever searched for satisfaction, completion, and fulfillment. Restless in that search, we have demonstrated throughout history that the more we struggle alone, the more we need love, cooperation, and unity.

We seem to fight a battle from birth, initially resisting every event that separates us from love—exile from the safety of the womb, loss of the mother's loving arms, the need, eventually, to leave home. Ever after, we strive to find unity in our individuality, while yearning to restore that missing love, safety, and sense of belonging in the universe. We try to feed our hunger for love through philosophy and religion, through romantic or sexual partners, through our lifestyles, or just through good-natured fellowship. When the deeper satisfaction does not come, we resort to war, seek different partners, enmesh ourselves in the ditraction of materialism, or lose ourselves in the numbness of drugs and alcohol.

Who would deny that we feel separate from each other and separate from our Creator? The faithful of the world's religions look toward their institutions to supply this absent unity. Modern psychology, barely a century old, works toward solving the mistakes of human emotion and the behavior that causes our misery, dissatisfaction, or emptiness. Psychologists attempt to explain our unhappiness with theories that range from repressed childhood trauma and unfulfilled needs to the cold mechanics of determinism. Yet, despite the rituals and theories, mistakes of human activity continue, because true satisfaction and inner completion seem always to be just beyond our reach—knowledge of our Creator just beyond our comprehension.

What is this drive for completeness—in all its safe, warm, forgiving comfort? Where is the solution to be found?

The truth is that we already possess the answer, right inside us. Know it or not, this completeness is alive wherever love stirs an ember or a flame. It is in the very commonality of the goodness that we each possess as we strive to preserve life, help a neighbor, cherish peace, or seek a better relationship with God. This book seeks, not just to explore that truth, but to lead the reader *directly into the heart of our remembrance of love* from which we have never wanted to separate.

"The Lord thy God is One," echoes from the pages of the world's scriptures. What can it mean, then, that we are created in God's image, if we are not also one with God and somehow one with each other? The answer to all these questions can be found in the truth of "oneness," and this book offers a lifeline—a golden thread of oneness—that can lead us to a deep understanding of oneness and our place in its midst. The reading of this book is intended to be "an experience of the heart," when read as an adventure, to invite us on a personal journey back to the beginning of creation itself. The book will then lead us deep within ourselves to the Universal Consciousness from which all knowledge flows and where we already possess the qualities we need to experience oneness. Furthermore, this book will reveal how understanding oneness can restore a missing sense of fulfillment and completion in our lives.

Oneness has been called the "universal theme" of the psychic readings of Edgar Cayce, America's best-documented clairvoyant, and specific references to his material will be invaluable for filling in the historical blanks and mysterious passages in scripture that seem to obscure our view of our true nature.

The Golden Thread of Oneness was written to lead the reader intuitively to a realization of our oneness in a step-by-step journey back to the very beginning of creation itself. The book will lead us to the deepest secrets of creation, the origin of the soul, and the story of how we came to separate ourselves from God. Along the way, we will discover many other sources that not only corroborate information in the readings, but add deeper significance to what we may already believe.

Further, the book offers simple but powerful exercises, based on the readings, for remembering our oneness with God and experiencing oneness in our lives. It emphasizes our oneness with God and with each other by leading us to the Universal Consciousness—the oneness of all thought that was accessed at will by Jesus Christ, Gautama Buddha, and all those who have called humankind back to the memory of its oneness with the Creator.

Humankind is now at a crossroads that many people believe is critical to the future of our evolution and survival. On a planetary scale, more and more people are seeking answers beyond the visible realm. Millions are experiencing a shift in consciousness that promises to bring our inherent knowledge of God closer to the surface—revealing the oneness that overflows the wells of our hungry hearts. It is the goal of this book to help everyone experience his or her oneness, to remove the separation that blocks our true spiritual growth, and to rediscover the miraculous tool of the Universal Consciousness for practical use in our daily lives.

Chapter 1

FINDING ONENESS IN A WORLD OF MANY

AN UNEXPECTED SCOLDING

On a chilly day in March, seven months before the stock market crash of 1929, stockbroker Morton Blumenthal arrived at the office of Edgar Cayce in Virginia Beach, Virginia. At age thirty-three, Mr. Blumenthal had already received hundreds of readings from the famous psychic. That day, however, he would be given a peculiar assignment, almost in the form of an order from the entranced Cayce.

The reading began normally enough, in the presence of Cayce's wife, Gertrude; Gladys Davis (the stenographer who recorded many of Cayce's readings verbatim); and Edgar Cayce's father, L.B. Cayce. Also in attendance was Mr. F. A. Van Patten, a real estate broker and early officer in the organization that would later become the Association for Research and Enlightenment (A.R.E.), which Cayce founded in 1931.

In typical fashion, Cayce began the reading with a general message for Mr. Blumenthal, which, in this case, seemed to chastise him. Though Cayce was always loving and helpful, in this reading he gently scolded Blumenthal in that many of the truths he had received through Cayce over the years had been "left aside" for more interesting pursuits. Cayce then admonished him to compile and correlate the advice he had received in his various readings, so that the information could be properly understood and applied.

Mr. Blumenthal and his associates were interested in helping the newly built Cayce Hospital to succeed, as well as in sharing the vast information of the readings with the world. To this end, he asked Cayce how he could better understand those with whom he was working. The reading advised him that in order to better understand his colleagues he had better understand *himself.*

(Q) Does this mean that I may study these experiences of these individuals—

(A) Rather of self—through the individuals' experiencing, applied to self and *how* to apply same to those that would hearken. (900-429)

Changing the subject, Mr. Blumenthal then asked how often he should give lectures or classes on the Cayce work in Virginia Beach, Virginia, the home of A.R.E. The compassionate source told him not to overtax himself, but then went on to say that, in his talks, he should attempt to deliver only a message that "gives life, light, and understanding." The source said to always try to help people "gain that same access to the Father as was made by the Son . . . "

The hardest task, complained Mr. Blumenthal to Edgar Cayce, was how to put the great fundamental principles in simple terms especially for people who sought scientific or religious evidence. Cayce's answer astounds us to this day. He said:

None is convinced in that science or religious convictions are one. The first lesson for *six months* should be *one*—One—One—*one;* Oneness of God, oneness of man's relation, oneness of force, oneness of time, oneness of purpose, *oneness* in every effort—Oneness—Oneness! (900-429)

It may never be known if this advice helped Mr. Blumenthal and his associates through the economic catastrophe that lurked just around the corner for the nation and much of the world, but the Cayce material makes it very clear, in hundreds of readings, that oneness is the key to success in our pursuits, both spiritual and mundane. According to many well-known Cayce scholars, oneness is the central theme of the Cayce readings.

JUST TO BELONG

"Man can will nothing unless he has first understood that he must count on no one but himself . . . !" The essence of loneliness was never better expressed than in this sad declaration by Jean-Paul Sartre in his *Being and Nothingness* (1943). He spoke for a generation of intellectuals who, upon observing the industrialization, warfare, and hedonism of the early twentieth century, erroneously concluded that we live in a universe without God. Still, as the century progressed, modern human beings, especially in the West, found themselves experiencing an isolation from each other, a loneliness within the crowd that had never before been known. Society continues to fragment, families to dissolve, and technology sometimes makes us feel like cogs in a machine or meaningless numbers on a list.

We have all experienced loneliness in one form or another. We know the feeling of being lonely in a crowded city or all alone on a deserted road. We have all felt alone, even amid the hilarity of a party. But from childhood, we all try to "belong" to someone or something. It is our nature to seek the company of others and, in them, enjoy a sense of belonging. Despite the dour declaration that provided meaning for the existentialists, we seek the pleasure of joining with others in conversation, work, play, love. We seek partners to work with, to live with, to marry. Many of us don't stop there—but we surround ourselves with more people, even if we have to create them in the form of children.

In all these activities, we are driven to *belong*. Yet, somehow, the outward trophies of our accomplishments do not fully satisfy us. While we can find temporary joys in our relationships, work, and material possessions, many of us often feel an inner impulse to belong to something even bigger, deeper. We believe that there is a God, yet we feel separate from God. Our churches so much as insist upon it. Even as adults, we yearn for the security we felt as little children, wishing that we could have heavenly parents to hold and comfort us in their arms.

In a reading given to a seventeen-year-old female student in 1944, Cayce addressed the issue of loneliness and gave advice that can help us all:

Thus we find an innate loneliness, an innate desire for companionship, that feeling that others are just a little bit better in their activities, that inferior something within self. But know, as has been given, if your ideal is set ye may so live as to be an example for many, and yet never be one of those who is so high and mighty as not to know that God is not a respecter of persons. He respects character, loveliness, kindness, patience, gentleness, brotherly love, and these manifested in thy experience will make thee a lovely person. (5256-1)

"God is not a respecter of persons" means that the show we

put on in the outer world of the personality has little lasting value, but that love, virtue, and everything of beauty that we generate from our inner character is lasting, in fact, is a part of God. The readings are clear that there is no difference in that inner character—the soul—from one person to the next. It is the same in each of us. At this level of inner beauty that we all possess, say the readings, we are one with each other and one with God.

Many scholars identify oneness as the central philosophy of Edgar Cayce's work. What it amounts to is discovering this oneness within:

One is the beginning, to be sure. Before *one* is nothing. After *one* is nothing, if all be *in one*—as *one* God, *one* Son, *one* Spirit. This, then, the *essence* of *all* force, *all* manners of energies. All activities *emanate* from the *one*. (5751-1)

What is this oneness about which Cayce's source spoke so dramatically, and why should we believe what the Cayce readings say about it? How can knowledge of oneness help us in the day-to-day living of our lives in this world of billions of people, this world of places, religions, governments, foods, ideas, flora, and fauna? The multiplicity of our world is even more apparent when we consider that within each of us flourishes the diversity of our own thoughts and feelings. How can we, ourselves, identify with a *oneness* about it all—a common ground that links everyone and everything?

The Cayce readings make the idea of oneness abundantly clear and, as is typical in the readings, show us how to "put [it] in practice by its practical application in the daily living . . . " (2771-1)

EDGAR CAYCE'S SOURCES

The Cayce readings comprise over 14,000 multipage readings that Cayce gave until his death at the age of sixty-seven in 1945. The size of the collection is eleven times the size of the Old and New Testaments combined—over 49,000 pages—and covers every imaginable topic from medical treatments to religion, from spiritual guidance to ancient history.

Cayce began giving psychic readings as a young man, and for years they focused on health topics for people who could find no relief through ordinary medicine. Cayce was a simple, self-educated, conservative Christian from Kentucky, who read the Bible once for every year of his life. As such, the responses to philosophical questions put to him were often surprising, both to those who were in attendance and to Cayce himself. After a reading was over, Cayce would awaken and have to be told what had been said during the reading, because he had been unconscious throughout the entire process.

Much has been written about just how Cayce's readings were possible. In his book, *Venture Inward,* Hugh Lynn Cayce, the mystic's eldest son, discusses how his father was able to give readings. The predominant explanation is that he made contact with a vast universal realm. Cayce himself gave his own explanation while speaking to a study group in 1933. He said, "There would seem to be not only one, but several sources of information that I tap." One of these sources, he said, was the subconscious of the individual for whom the reading was being given. In the case of physical readings, a "cooperative effort" between the minds of Cayce and the recipient seemed to be at work. Other sources, although considerably less frequent, included what appears to have been highly advanced spiritual entities and departed souls who participated in order to impart specific help.

Psychologist Henry Reed, Ph.D., in *Your Mind: Unlocking Your Hidden Powers,* refers to Cayce's ability to enter a "superconscious trance state," and even to "travel back in time." Reed goes on to say that from a "state of infinite knowing," Cayce claimed that everyone has the ability to do what he did. All knowledge, state the Cayce readings, is within. "Inside our own minds." This Universal Consciousness, or superconscious mind, was by far the most frequent source of Cayce's work.

All force is as one force. Hence the universal forces. All knowledge is as one knowledge. Hence may be attained from the universal force or knowledge. (254-30)

Certain readings indicate that Cayce was actually able to "read" from a celestial book—the Akashic Record—where all thoughts and deeds are recorded in a nonphysical dimension of consciousness. The readings often refer to the "book of thy remembrance" or "God's book of remembrance." The Akashic Record is:

The record that the individual entity itself writes upon the skein of time and space, through patience—and is opened when self has attuned to the infinite, and may be read by those attuning to that consciousness. (2533-8)

If this is the case, then all memory and all knowledge are one. Nothing that is thought, said, or done is ever lost, and we all have access to this knowledge if we attune to the consciousness of the infinite. The primary source that Cayce accessed, therefore, was some unified field of knowledge to which everyone can attune and which, he said in the following reading, is the Universal Consciousness, or God:

What is thy God, then? Is it self, fame, fortune? or is it that which is of the creative influence that is of the universal consciousness ye call God, Jehovah, Father? (2796-1)

This message is repeated in many readings, and Cayce allows no misunderstanding that each of us is one with the whole. One in body, mind, and spirit with the Creator. It has ever been thus and will always be, and the proof reaches around the world and in nearly every spiritual tradition.

Hidden deep within us lies a primordial awareness or common memory of our creation and of our original oneness with God. Perhaps this memory is encoded in our DNA or slumbers quietly in our subconscious minds. But if oneness is the underlying truth of all things, rediscovering it should be our most joyful pursuit, if not our supreme duty. The Cayce readings tell us that we can not only reawaken that knowledge, but we eventually must, if we are to find solutions for the problems of our planet and the frustrations in our own lives. Luckily for us, we have a built-in mechanism by which we can know oneness. It's a "golden thread" of memory that tethers us to the Universal Consciousness—a thread that we will follow closely as the chapters of this book unfold.

ONENESS IN DIVERSITY

Browse through an outline of human history and a paradox of trends appears. History is certainly littered with the corpses of war. One could speculate on which wars were wars of defense or aggression, but our record, as the "children of God," seems to have been a bumpy one. Even now, the persistence of war is baffling.

But we can observe yet another trend that lifts our view to a more optimistic promontory. Despite our wars, we can observe movements, whether voluntary or unavoidable, toward cohesion, peace, and unity. As our modern world finds itself having no choice but to cooperate and work as an international unit, we shouldn't be surprised to discover that this movement has been with us all along.

Even before the Bronze Age, separate individuals colluded into families, families into villages, villages into communities, and communities into nations. In our modern world, clear political and economic boundaries are vanishing as the developing nations are being absorbed by the world of wealth, commerce, and technology. Yet, Europe has banded together economically and politically into the European Union. *Newsweek* magazine (February 17, 1997) reports that the European nations, in fact, are expected to be using a single currency, called the "Euro," by 2002. The United Nations takes the entire world under its protective wing, even as its efficiency is under debate.

Earnest ecumenical religious conferences now include a broad spectrum of spiritual traditions. Many people anticipate a positive new world order, while some hope for a "one-world government" and a "one-world religion." Whether these visions materialize or not, large groups of people now rally for everything from civil rights, to animal rights, to environmental reform. Like each individual, each nation on the earth plays its unique role in the whole of human activity, whereas at the level of spirit we hold our basic values, our biology, and our very consciousness in common. Concepts from Eastern religions, metaphysical research, and mystical thought are slowly awakening people to the idea that none of us is superior to another, whether for patriotism, creed, gender, or color of skin, but that we are all equally loved in the mind of God.

Despite the apparent diversity of the world's sociopolitical and theological differences, therefore, something deep within us makes us want to pull together for our common fundamental goals. This brings into focus the paradox of how oneness can be possible in the midst of, or in spite of, such diversity. In order to solve the paradox, perhaps we need to look more closely at the qualities that make us the same, because, even though we are unique individuals, we are bound to our singular choice to choose a path back to oneness with God.

The human race is certainly linked through biology. We all breathe air; our brains perceive phenomena and process information; and we all need food to live. Scientists tell us that every element is present in our bodies, and Cayce takes this concept a giant step further:

For within the human body—living, not dead—*living* human forces—we find every element, every gas, every mineral, every influence that is outside of the organism itself. For indeed it is one with the whole. (470-22)

Our biology is one, but what about our similarities at the level of thought? The famous words of René Descartes inexorably link us together, for humankind, whether as individuals or all together, shines as one in the instant of, "I think, therefore, I am." This is true from the loftiest mathematician down to the lowliest pickpocket. In our daily lives, we humans reason, solve problems, and use languages. In groups, we invent governments and establish trade with others. Despite our apparent differences, humankind the world over already shares in oneness. Our journey through life would seem to be a continuous discovery of diversity, apparently infinite in scope. But in truth, our task—and we will discover that it can be a simple one, if we choose to make it so—is to identify ourselves with the oneness in diversity.

In *Desert Wisdom: Sacred Middle Eastern Writings from the Goddess Through the Sufis,* author Neil Douglas-Klotz offers his inspired new translations of texts ranging from the Old and New Testaments to the revered poetry of Rumi. The following translation of a *hadith* (recorded saying) of the prophet Muhammad shines a revealing light in places of the human heart that seem to be long asleep:

> *Cosmic Unity has seventy thousand ways to hide.*
>
> *The One Being wraps itself in countless disguises:*
> *It veils itself in light and darkness,*
> *in appearance and disappearance,*
> *in sage guidance,*
> > *a torch to understanding,*
> *and in foolish advice,*
> > *the extinction of wisdom.*
>
> *In the rising and setting of enlightenment.*
>
> *One moment we shield our eyes from the glare,*
> > *the next we shudder in shadow.*
> *Eclipse and Brilliance both obscure from mind's view*
> > *the Universe's single-minded purpose.*

In the case of oneness, simplicity is the key to understanding the complex. All thought, even paradox, is a product of the mind and, therefore, is contained therein.

If oneness is the law and all is truly one, how can we know it or experience it for ourselves? By what law or capability can we raise our awareness, so that we can become conscious of this oneness and remember our original oneness with God when we were created? The truth is that not a day goes by without that oneness nudging us, tugging at our hand, or turning our head. These "urges from the unseen," as the readings call them, are nothing less than the love of God trying to seep into our resistive habits, which is also known as the gift of "grace."

WHEN THINGS GO RIGHT

In the spring of 1989, my wife and I were living in Charleston, South Carolina. The charming, historic city had been our home for six years, but the time had come to make some important life decisions. By that spring, our financial situation had become a serious problem. In the fall of 1986, I had been laid off, along with everyone else on the staff, from my job at a local theater company. I'd struggled to survive by writing feature stories for local newspapers and magazines, and by writing play scripts for local producers, but it wasn't enough. My wife, Robin, who had worked as a chef in several downtown restaurants, had been forced by physical exhaustion to sacrifice her career—and salary. By May, we were not only broke, but deeply in debt.

I'd spent the winter months hunting for work in theater and for magazine jobs from Atlanta to Charlotte, but to little avail. Our concern grew from worry to panic. Finally, we just didn't know what to do.

Like many people, we'd always done our best praying when life got rough. Like Abraham Lincoln once said, "I've often found myself on my knees in prayer, because it had become apparent that I had nowhere else to go." We had no other choices and no more ideas, so we gave our situation to God to solve and, fingers crossed, shrugged helplessly.

On May 25, the beginning of Charleston's famous Spoleto Festival of music and arts—a festival that had always given me extra work with my former employer—I had a strange dream. I saw three camels at the Battery—the oak-lined, moss-draped park that overlooks the harbor with its famous Fort Sumter in the distance. The camels were standing there, while someone was digging a deep hole in the ground. That was all I remembered when I awoke, and to this day I don't know what the symbols meant. However, I also heard a very strong message in my head: You have to get out of Charleston right away!

Well, this wasn't anything we didn't already know. But my description of the dream prompted an immediate inspiration from my wife.

The year before, we had visited the A.R.E. in Virginia Beach to do some research in the library there. With the trip now long forgotten, Robin suddenly said: "Why don't you call the A.R.E., and see if they need a writer?"

I told her that I was in no mood for jokes, but after two days of her cajoling, I agreed. The A.R.E. did, in fact, need a writer. I applied. I was called in for an interview, and by June 6, 1989, we had moved to Virginia Beach and I was a full-time employee.

When I received word that A.R.E. had hired me, we sat back in wonder and amazement, because it had only been a few days since we decided to give our insurmountable problem to God. We had stopped worrying and panicking. We were feeling very centered, calm, and quiet in our hearts. We had been, inexplicably, feeling at-one within ourselves, with each other, and with the universe. And out of that quiet peace, the solution had been handed to us on a silver platter: though me, in a dream, and through Robin as startling inspiration.

Most of us have had the experience of finally finding solutions to problems by "letting go and letting God." This concept is an important clue to our rediscovery of oneness: by giving ourselves over to the will of God, we give up our precious arrogance. We float out into the deep part of the river of Universal Consciousness, where guidance is abundant and free.

UNIVERSAL CONSCIOUSNESS

Consciousness is difficult to describe or define, because we are never without it. Consciousness, basically, is *everything*. It is the eternal flame of awareness, and it is also our eternal presence in the endless "now." The flame does not go out, not even when we are asleep or when our bodies die. Definitions of consciousness, whether they come from psychology or religion, range from the abstract to the simplistic. Exploring a handful of the most widely believed ones, however, can help us acquire the best definition of all: the one based on our own informed observations.

Psychiatrist Carl Jung suggested that consciousness maintains the relation of "psychic contents to the ego; distinguished conceptually from the psyche, which encompasses both consciousness and the unconscious." He also believed that consciousness cannot create itself, that "it wells up from unknown depths."

The Eastern religions of ancient origins tend to divide consciousness into levels and aspects, which can be studied, analyzed, clarified, and mastered through meditation and other disciplines. From the yogic traditions of India, we receive a view that consciousness is transcendental of this world, of our bodies, and our lives. The yogis propose consciousness as the "ultimate identity of human beings."

J. Donald Walters was one of Paramahansa Yogananda's first students. In his book, *Superconsciousness: A Guide to Meditation*, he writes that "Consciousness, in its pure state, is absolute: more absolute than the speed of light, which slows on entering a material medium such as the earth's atmosphere; more absolute than the existence of matter, which is only a manifestation of energy; more absolute than energy, which is itself a vibration of consciousness." On the other hand, according to Tibetan Buddhist Chögyam Trungpa, in *The Myth of Freedom and the Way of Meditation*, consciousness consists of "emotions and irregular thought patterns, all of which, taken together, form the different fantasy worlds with which we occupy ourselves."

The Edgar Cayce readings define consciousness in various ways. "What then *is* thy mind?" asks reading 826-11. "The gift of God, that is the companion with thy soul, that is a part of same!" In reading 3744-2, the conscious mind is described as that which "is the active force in an animate object; that is the spark, or image of the Maker" and that which "is able to be manifested in the physical plane through one of the senses." (The readings' view of consciousness, as well as the other levels of the mind, will be discussed in chapters 5 and 6.)

A detailed comparison of these various concepts of consciousness is fascinating, though complex. Yet, with these few examples, we can begin to approach an experience of oneness through the Universal Consciousness. The Cayce readings actually contain 381 references to "Universal Consciousness," such as:

For, each soul and the spirit thereof is a part of that Universal Consciousness or God. (2282-1)

For, the entity was ever a part of the Universal Consciousness, but was given the will—which is the birthright of each soul that it might be individual knowing itself to be itself and yet one with the Creative Forces. (2524-1)

For, as indicated oft, each entity has within itself the possibilities of the Universal Consciousness. (3685-1)

Like oneness, the dynamic influence of the Universal Consciousness pervades our experiences every day. It's easy to identify, too, especially in our mundane lives. We spend most of our lives exercising our personalities, the body-mind level of consciousness, dealing with emotions, problems, and routine human concerns. But our consciousness occasionally dips into the universal river, such as happened to Robin and me in the story above. This occurs as we weave into and out of proximity to the Universal Consciousness, which, as the readings show, is God. We can begin to make contact more purposefully with the Universal Consciousness once we realize that we belong to a great loving universe, and that our original oneness with God is still present and waiting for us to find it again.

The Cayce readings make it plain that we are not only capable of it, we are a part of it. We can't really escape it, although we *can* ignore it. Reading 1096-4 states: "Not that . . . the entity hasn't its own free will, but it—the entity or soul—develops either to a oneness with that Universal Consciousness or in opposition to same." (1096-4)

As always, therefore, we have a choice, and we will discuss various aspects of the choices we make as we trace the golden thread of our oneness with God and with each other. According to the religious traditions of the world, this experience is closer than we think.

WINDOWS ON ONENESS FROM THE EDGAR CAYCE READINGS

Oneness of Good
For, know that life is continuous, as is good. All temporal desire or purpose *must* pass away. Only the good, the true, the spiritually beautiful, live on. (2594-1)

Oneness of the Soul
Thus does the hope of eternal life, the hope that is innate within, spring ever anew within the human breast. For *only* in man is there the existence of the soul that is not just universal, but individual; capable of becoming as a god, as one with the Creative Forces. (1587-1)

Oneness of Life
For, life is the manifestation of that force ye call God, in whatever form it may appear; and is *one!* (2505-1)

Oneness of Force
All force, all power that is manifested in the earth, *emanates* from a spiritual or God-force . . . (815-3)

Oneness of Humankind
One finds self a body, a mind, a soul; each with its own attributes and its activity in the earth. An entity, then, is a pattern of that which is also a spiritual fact; Father, Son, Holy Spirit. These are one, just as an individual entity is one. An entity, then, is the pattern of divinity in materiality, or in the earth. (3357-2)

Oneness of Time
For, while time and space are literal only to the consciousness of the finite mind, they are a part of the experience in materiality; and the presentations of same then should be of creative forces—as time, space, patience. For with the creating of these came the consciousness of being separated from Creative Forces, or God. (2000-3)

Oneness of Purpose
For the purpose of each soul's entrance into materiality is to be a channel of blessings to others. (1604-1)

Oneness of Relationships
All may be of one mind, however, and yet not think the same thoughts. All may be in unison of purpose and yet apparently separate in their activity. (2992-1)

Chapter 2

THE LORD THY GOD IS ONE

TRUTH IS ONE, THE PATHS ARE MANY

In 1958, religion scholar Huston Smith, Ph.D., published his now famous book, *The Religions of Man*, which sought to concisely examine the meanings within the world's major religions. "What a strange fellowship this is," he writes. "The God-seekers of every clime, lifting their voices in the most diverse ways imaginable to the God of all men. How does it all sound to Him? Like bedlam? Or, in some mysterious way, does it blend into harmony?"

In the previous chapter, we looked at evidence of oneness and also at an intriguing paradox: there are myriad differences among the world's people, and yet there are many commonalities, both mundane and conceptual, that bind us all together. Trends in this world of international cooperation now range across political, economic, sexual, and even religious boundaries. In the words of Huston Smith, "We have come to the point in history when anyone who is only a Japanese or only an American, only an Oriental or only a Westerner, is but half human; the other half of his being which beats with the pulse of all mankind has yet to be born."

Our differences, therefore, are all too easy to see. It is the other half of our being that remains a mystery—the "lasting" part that we share with each other and with God—our oneness. This is the part that is eternal, immortal. It is the soul. Despite the many divisions that separate the world's religions and the schisms that splinter them from within, a closer look strangely reveals their oneness. We are, in truth, spiritually all alike.

Edgar Cayce encouraged the study of the religions of others and expressed the conclusion in this way:

... coordinate the teachings, the philosophies of the East and the West, the Oriental and the Occidental, the new truths and the old ... Correlate not the differences, but where all religions meet—*there is one God!* "Know, O Israel, the Lord thy God is one!" (991-1)

However remote we may now feel from the reality of oneness, our understanding steps into a brighter light when we realize how the oneness of God is vibrantly alive in the religions of the world.

As different as they seem from each other and despite the wars those differences have fostered over the centuries, it is the one-ness of God that binds together the people of Judaism, Christianity, and Islam—the "Descendants of Abraham." What links these religions together is primarily the Pentateuch, or the first five books of the Bible, which they all acknowledge. In Judaism this body of writing is called the Torah and to Jews it comprises "the Law," the central living teaching of Judaism. God's gift to the Descendants of Abraham—oneness instead of many—was a necessary step for their spiritual birth and survival.

According to Jewish theology, the human mind cannot fully encompass God. It asserts that God is immutable and an "un-fathomable totality." This unfathomable totality of God is iden-tified in kabbalah (mystical Judaism) as *Ain Soph*—the "infinite." At the level of *Ain Soph*, God is the entire endless sphere of the universe, but also the dimensionless point in its center. *Ain Soph* contains the Tree of Life, which is depicted as the ten divine at-tributes of God and the ten aspects of human consciousness. God's oneness, however, remains indivisible in Judaism, and, as we shall see, this oneness is a mystical truth that unifies all the major religions at their common core.

Christianity, of course, maintained the precept of the one God as its foundation, and Jesus Christ taught the principle through-out His life (see "Jesus Taught Oneness" later in this chapter). The Tree of Life helps Jews understand aspects of God in more hu-man terms, and Christians augment their understanding of God with the concept of a "trinity"—Father, Son, and Holy Spirit. But Christians, too, maintain the indivisibility of the oneness of God. The New Testament frequently refers to this, and Paul expresses it beautifully:

There is one body and one Spirit, just as you were called to the one hope that belongs to your call, one Lord, one faith, one baptism, one God and Father of us all, who is above all and through all and in all. (Ephesians 4:4-6)

Belief in the one God—*Allah* in Arabic—is also a fundamental concept of Islam. The Koran, in fact, supports the validity of the Pentateuch (see the Koran, 3:3; 5:15, 48; 35:31). The Jews, after all, are the descendants of Abraham through Isaac, whereas the Muslims are the descendants of Abraham through Ishmael. During various periods in Jewish history, adoption of false gods interfered in their relationship with Yahweh. By the sixth century A.D., however, the Meccans, too, had allowed superstitions, gods, and jinni (genies) to crowd Allah out. Muhammad was born, it seems, just in time to save his people from rampant disorder, bloodshed, and licentiousness. He did this by writing down God's words in the Koran and teaching its *suras* (chapters) to them. Through Muhammad, Allah gave the descendants of Ishmael rules to live by and reestablished in them the truth that Allah is one. Muhammad did acknowledge a deep appreciation for Jesus and His prophetic message, although he did not recognize a literal resurrection.

The oneness of God is a theme in dozens of religions the world over. In Zoroastrianism, the pre-Islamic religion of Persia (Iran), God is called *Ahura Mazda* and is the one true God, the creator of the world and all that is good. Like Abraham, Moses, and Muhammad, its founder, Zoroaster, unified a people who had also given themselves over to many gods. The Zoroastrian sacred scriptures, the *Zend Avesta*, is identified in the readings as "also from that same one who gave, 'I am the way, the truth and the light.'" (3685-1) The readings advised at least one individual to study these teachings:

The entity came and made for those conditions that brought to its own land a greater peace and harmony, and aided in the establishing of what later became the Zoroastrian activity; which has in the present been of especial interest—and will be more so if it is studied the more. (815-2)

In China, we find Taoism, which defines itself as "the Way." Based on a little book attributed to Lao-Tsu, the *Tao Teh Ching*, Taoism does not identify God by name, yet defines the Tao as "the way of *ultimate reality*." The Tao, therefore, is oneness, at its essence, because the Tao includes everything.

From the aboriginal myth of the "dream time" to the Great Spirit of the Native Americans, no people whose religion survives has escaped God's message of oneness, whether through their prophets, saints, or their medicine men and women. However, as we trace this message, we sometimes have to look beyond the way we see a religion practiced today and examine the essence of its original principles.

This is especially true in the case of Hinduism, which is a tolerant religion because it acknowledges the existence of many paths to God, not just its own. India is a nation which recognizes sixteen official languages and in which seven major religions are practiced—Hinduism, Buddhism, Islam, Christianity, Sikhism, Sufism, and Parsis (Zoroastrianism). Hinduism, with all of its observable social problems, tolerates these other religions as being equally valid quests for truth. Many people are baffled by the crowded pantheon of Hindu mythology and tend to dismiss Hinduism as a religion of "many gods." However, the Vedas (India's most ancient scriptures from which Hinduism evolved) contain a phrase, "Truth is one; sages call it by different names."

THE TRUE NAME

Hinduism brings the "unfathomable totality" of God, called *brahman* (immensity) in Sanskrit, into more human terms by personifying its various aspects. As we have seen, Christianity attributes a trinity of aspects to God, and Judaism has ten divine aspects. Out of the abstract, impersonal immensity *(brahman)*, Brahma (Immense-Being) is the creator of the visible universe, the world, and of life. Vishnu is the one who lights, sustains, and maintains the created universe, and Shiva represents darkness and the aspect of God that destroys fragile physical creation. The hundreds of other aspects of the divine and the representative gods that Hindus worship seem overwhelming in terms of number and complication to non-Hindus, but there is an easy way to perceive the oneness behind it all.

Alain Daniélou, in his book, *The Myths and Gods of India*, explains it this way: "The Hindu, whether he be a worshiper of the Pervader (Vishnu), the Destroyer (Shiva), Energy (Shakti), or the Sun (Surya), is always ready to acknowledge the equivalence of these deities as the manifestations of distinct powers springing from [that] unknowable 'Immensity.'"

Within us is *atman*—the soul, which is a part of *Atman*, the universal soul. According to Hinduism, we can become *one* with *brahman* through the disciplines of our spiritual path of choice. "Whoever worships any divinity other than the Immensity," says the *Brahadanyaka Upanishad* (1.4.10), "thinking 'He is one and I another,' he knows not."

Sufism is the name most often applied to Islamic mysticism, the roots of which actually predate Muhammad. The basis of Sufi philosophy is that we can have direct experience with and knowledge of God. It promotes the idea of the *immediate personal union* of the soul with God. Not only do Sufis accept oneness, they insist that we have never been anything *but* one with God. Through their various practices, such as dancing and praying together in groups, they are able to experience this oneness in their conscious minds.

Sikhism, a combination of devotional Hinduism and mystical Islam (especially Sufism), was founded in the 1400s by Nanak, who wrote the *Adi Granth*, or *Original Book*. Dissatisfied with the separation of the Hindu and Islamic gods, he declared them to be one and the same, being the ultimate reality, uncreated and eternal, identified simply as "The True Name."

Sikhs silently read the following Creed each day:

There is but one God whose name is True, the Creator, devoid of fear and enmity, immortal, unborn, self-existent, great and bountiful. The True One was in the beginning, the True One was in the primal age. The True One is, was, O Nanak, and the True One also shall be.

Seemingly all by itself in its mystery and abstractions, Buddhism holds the doctrine of the "not-self," denying the personality completely and disavowing the existence of any personalized God or, in fact, personalized human being. Buddhism is thought of as atheistic in the West, but even though it exacts no laws or dogmas, this is far from the truth. According to Dorothy C. Donath, author of *Buddhism for the West*, it "teaches unity with all life everywhere, and compassion for every living being, man and animal alike . . . " Buddhism's principle of *ahimsa*, harmlessness to all sentient life, is its firm belief that there is oneness in all life.

The Cosmos, according to Buddhism, is a manifestation of pure Mind—consciousness—again, the "unfathomable totality" of Judaism that has no beginning and no end. Buddhism has been called a teaching for the intellect, a universal teaching that strives to dissolve illusion *(maya)* so that the ultimate reality—elsewhere known as Universal Consciousness, or "God"—can be perceived. Through self-discipline, anyone can awaken to this reality, just as Siddhartha Gautama did when he became "awake" as the Buddha. The enlightened state of Buddhahood leads to Nirvana—an intellectually indescribable state of being (implying Oneness with Bliss)—which, according to Huston Smith, is as close as Buddhism comes to identifying a personalized God, but which is exquisite in its description of the ethical effects of oneness.

Buddhists embrace the concept of oneness in many ways. To them, everything is sacred, and everyone and everything are worthy of compassion. Tibetan Buddhist priest and author, Kalu Rinpoche, offers these observations about how oneness manifests in our world:

All appearance is a form of divinity, all sound is the sound of mantra [prayer], and all thought and awareness is the divine play of transcending awareness.

To further illustrate oneness, John Powers, author of *An Introduction to Tibetan Buddhism,* relates the story of a lama who managed to escape the invading Chinese. He traveled to northern India where he hid himself as a construction worker for several years. Finally, he was recognized by one of his former students, who could not believe that such an important lama was doing menial labor. Had he revealed his identity, the student said, the lama would have been able to live in comfort in a monastery surrounded by adoring students.

The lama replied that, for him, there was no difference between working on roads and living in a monastery. He explained that when he shoveled dirt, he visualized it as pure offerings that he gave to Buddha. Moving heavy boulders symbolized his struggle to remove recalcitrant mental afflictions. And his fellow workers were fully enlightened buddhas whose actions were performed for his benefit.

Through the lama's attitude, he had made his world pure, holy, and free from negative thoughts by being "one" with it all, whatever happened to him. Our own eventual, inevitable realization of our oneness with God, oneness within ourselves, and oneness with each other will surely resemble this attitude. It is a message that is repeated often in the Cayce readings:

Yet remember, "the Lord thy God is one Lord!" O that man

**would but attain to that consciousness and apply that principle
in his dealings with every activity! (5142-1)**

It is clear, then, from even a brief examination of some of the
world's religions, that the concept of oneness pervades throughout. Somehow, through his prophets, God has brought into the
world's centers of thought and guidance a reminder to people
that God—Universal Consciousness—is the ultimate reality and
that God is One. The teachings, gospels, verses, sutras, and suras
all strive to teach us how to deal with distraction, temptation,
and the illusions and delusions of this world. This is so that we
can remain steadfast in our adherence to the oneness of God—
and that when we forget this fact, chaos, war, and unhappiness
can often be the result, both on our planet as well as in our individual lives.

JESUS TAUGHT ONENESS

The Cayce readings have much to say about the teachings of
Jesus. In terms of the religions of the world, Cayce was once
asked if Jesus had had anything to do with the development of
Buddhism, Islam, Confucianism, Shintoism, Hinduism, Platoism,
or Judaism. Cayce answered by saying, "As has been indicated,
the entity [Jesus]—as an entity—influenced either directly or in-
directly all those forms of philosophy or religious thought that
taught God was One." (364-9)

In the New Testament, Jesus often quoted the Old Testament
to establish the theme of oneness. He demonstrated our oneness, not only with Himself, but with the Father. In answer to His
questioners, Jesus explained the great commandment that had
been given by Moses (Deuteronomy 6:4-5): "The first is, *'Hear, O
Israel: The Lord our God, the Lord is one;* and you shall love the
Lord your God with all your heart, and with all your soul, and
with all your mind, and with all your strength.'" Jesus then gives
us a powerful clue to our oneness with God—a rather metaphysical notion—when He states the second greatest commandment
of all: "The second is this, *'You shall love your neighbor as yourself.'*There is no other commandment greater than these." (Mark
12:29-31) [italics added] Essentially, Jesus affirmed that God is
one and that to love our neighbor *is* to love God. This is a valuable key to discovering oneness within ourselves and each other.
It is also the key to Universal Consciousness, as we will discover.

But there is more. Jesus identified *Himself* as being one with God when He said: "I and the Father are one." (John 10:30) After He said this, some of those present picked up stones to stone Him. He asked them why, and they accused Him of sacrilege: that He was making Himself God. Quoting from Isaiah 41:23 and Psalm 82:6, Jesus answered them by saying, "Is it not written in your law, 'I said, you are gods'?" (John 10:34)

This is yet another confirmation of our oneness with God. Later, however, Jesus made the connection easy for us by speaking these words: "In that day *you will know* that I am in my Father, and you in me, and I in you." (John 14:20) [italics added]

In Vedic texts, we read statements that are almost identical to this:

"That which is I is he, that which is he is I." (*Katha Upanishad* 5.1)

"They are in me and I in them." (*Bhagavad Gita* 9.29)

This should come as no surprise to those who know from the Cayce readings that Jesus spent a number of years studying in India, as well as in Egypt and Persia. (There is more on this in chapter 4.)

Jesus often prayed to the Father, and oneness was frequently His underlying message. For example, He declared that, as He was one with us, He had glory with the Father from the beginning, "before the world was made." (John 17:5)

... that they may all be one; even as thou, Father, art in me, and I in thee, that they also may be in us, so that the world may believe that thou hast sent me. The glory which thou hast given me I have given to them, that they may be one even as we are one, I in them and thou in me, that they may become perfectly one, so that the world may know that thou hast sent me and hast loved them even as thou hast loved me. (John 17:21-23)

As we continue to search for firsthand knowledge of this inherent oneness in our lives, we receive other clues from Cayce, who points us always toward Christ:

Thus the records of each entity are a part of the Universal Consciousness ... For, as the spirit of the Christ is one, and the individual entity in its manifestations of thought, purpose and desire makes its awareness one with that consciousness, so may that soul awareness come. (2246-1)

Tracing the golden thread of oneness, we will return to the

teachings of Jesus, especially when we begin looking at practical ways by which we can regain our Universal Consciousness. In the meantime, Cayce reading 391-4 offers a helpful insight. It was given in November 1932 to a twenty-one-year-old male athlete. He had a number of questions concerning his health, his digestion in particular, and this would be his fourth reading from Edgar Cayce. Through Cayce's trancelike state, the sources gave him specific remedies and advice. The young man received quite an interesting response, however, when he asked what changes may have come into his spiritual life since his last reading:

Know that the Creative Energy called God may be as personal as an individual will allow same to be; for the Spirit is in the image of the Creative Forces and seeks manifestation. It may take that personality, that will be allowed by the individual itself; for we are colaborers, cocreators with that Energy we call God, that Energy we call Universal Forces. While this may appear to be the Whole, if we will understand that "The Lord thy God is *one*" and all power, all force emanates from that One Source, we will get an understanding of ourselves and our abilities. *Know self!* Be *true* to *self*, and ye will not be false to anyone! (391-4)

The Cayce readings often warned people that the bane of our existence is selfishness, wasteful thinking, and destructive behavior. "Spirit is the life, mind the builder, and the physical the result," the readings say, and to ignore this axiom is to invite discord within the mind and the body. This means that even as God first conceived us and the universe, everything that we ourselves create is first conceived in our minds. The objective is in our motivation:

If it is for self-expression, self-indulgence, self-glorification, self-gratification, the inclinations become in a direction away from, and not toward an at-onement with, the Whole. (2079-1)

So far, the golden thread has led us to certain discoveries: at some conscious or unconscious level, we have been one with the Father and Christ from the beginning. But if this is so, why is there such conflict in our lives, our world, and our minds? The answer lies within us, say the Cayce readings:

Within self, within [lie] the abilities to eradicate this, that or the other influence that *separates* the inner self from being aware of the oneness of all force and power that manifests itself in the earth ... (903-23)

It seems that where our mistakes are concerned, as well as our triumphs, we are the captains of our fate. By our erroneous actions and thoughts, we separate ourselves from God. The fact is, we began to feel this separation very early in the history of the human race. It is the cause of all the illusion with which humanity tortures itself and from which the religions of the world would free us by reminding us of the oneness of God and *our* oneness *in* God.

WHY DO WE FEEL SEPARATE?

The evidence of oneness, it seems, has been right in front of us, all along, but so is the evidence of our separateness from God. After all, many of us believe that we have only periodic access to God; for example, when we need to pray for help, when we are in church, and, if we're lucky, at some point after the body expires. Most of us live with the faith that God exists and identify certain earthly charms and events as having divine origins, while we regard others as being synthetic or not real. Not only do we feel separate from God, we also feel separate from each other—after all, how can I be you and how can you be me? How can capitalist Americans be one with communist Chinese, or Nigerians be one with the French?

As we explored in the previous chapter, our differences—the evidence of our separation—are abundant. We look different, speak different languages, and have different views on every aspect of our lives. There is paradox and diversity in everything. Life *and* death. Darkness *and* light. Good *and* evil. Mountains *and* valleys. There are stars *and* planets. Blue eyes *and* brown eyes. Gardens *and* deserts. In the range of human thought and emotion, there are ups and downs, baffling experiences that defy explanation. So, how did this sense of our separation from oneness come about?

The Cayce readings show that we actually chose to make ourselves separate. Furthermore, that we began to make those choices at the beginning itself, before the world was. One of the most overlooked statements about separation can be found in the difficult opening passages of Genesis in which God created the first duality: God created light, and then "separated" it from the darkness. The Cayce readings equate the "darkness and the light" to consciousness:

Then, in the mental plane, what becomes Day and Night? That which separates the one from the other. Or, as illustrated, the Day becomes the first day of the consciousness of separation from the forces which the power, or the activity, is in action. (262-56)

Originally created as "one" in God's image, we became cocreators in the universe when we received consciousness and free will. This was *because* our consciousness started out as God's consciousness—Universal Consciousness. We were one with thought itself, which had not yet fragmented into a myriad of our own ideas by which we would create individualized separation from God. It was our very self-awareness and turning our attention to the amusements we could enjoy in the material plane that helped this separation extend itself:

As given from the beginning, by becoming aware in a material world *is*—or was—the only manner or way through which spiritual forces might become aware of their separation from the spiritual atmosphere, the spiritual surroundings, of the Maker. (262-56)

It was, in fact, our own creations and our *desire* to be separate that led to the slow, steady forgetting of God and our innate divine oneness with God. We lost our direct connection to the divine when we created division. Like the blind leading the blind, we became lost in what we were creating: the thought forms, the games, experiments, beauty, pleasure, self-power, self-glorification, the creation and acquisition of materials, and the invention of tools and weapons.

Separation continued the more deeply we identified with the material plane—our place of self-chosen exile:

What has been given as the truest of all that has ever been written in Scripture? "God does not will that any soul should perish!" But man, in his headstrongness, harkens oft to that which would separate him from his Maker! (262-56)

We all know the biblical story of the Tower of Babel at the time when the "whole world had one language," (Genesis 11:1) in which the inhabitants decided to build a city and a tower whose top would reach heaven. When the Lord visited the city, however, He was displeased at what He saw:

And the LORD said, "Behold, they are one people, and they have all one language; and this is only the beginning of what they will do; and nothing that they propose to do will now be

impossible for them. Come, let us go down, and there confuse their language, that they may not understand one another's speech." (Genesis 11:6-7)

Due to our arrogance, we tried to create a kingdom of our own that was separate from God. The Lord then scattered us about the face of the earth, leaving us to suffer the effects of our own folly.

The readings identify this time as among "those first separations" (2460-1) after Noah's ark came to rest on dry land. Essentially, humankind had defied God in the earth, and the Tower of Babel is an allegory for the confusion that then arose among the people. It was, according to the readings, "the beginnings of nations." (3976-29) From separation, we would suffer, say the readings, and from suffering, we would learn:

. . . all souls in the beginning were one with the Father. The separation, or turning away, brought evil. Then there became the necessity of the awareness of self's being out of accord with, or out of the realm of blessedness; and, as given of the Son, "yet learned he obedience through the things which he suffered." (262-56)

As we will see in the following chapters, the subject of separation is an important one, because we need to understand it in order to free ourselves from our continuing separation from God. But first, we will travel back in time along the golden thread that God has spun for us over countless millennia. We will trace it through the prophets, the miracles, and the fascinating unseen records of oneness, leading to the first burst of creation itself.

ON THE ROAD TO CREATION

The suggestion that we can remember back to the time of our creation may, at first, seem ridiculous and impossible. Yet, we can truly retrace the journey through the world's scriptures and myths, filling in, as we go, from reliable spiritual records such as the Edgar Cayce readings. It would only delay our purpose to recount the stories and myths in detail, as we would become quickly mired in their sheer number. However, in order to get started, we will briefly look at a few of them.

Most of the Descendants of Abraham—Christians, Jews, and Muslims—take the creation story in Genesis 1:1 at face value: "In the beginning God created the heavens and the earth." The fact is stated without explanation as to who or what God is. The bizarre allegories of the Hindu *Mahabharata* tell of a goddess who gives birth to the planet from her womb. The Egyptians give us the story of Atum (The Complete One), who rose up out of chaos and created the earth. (In the next chapter, we will look more closely at the role ancient Egypt played in carrying the concept of oneness forward in human thought.)

The similarities among the world's creation stories are amazing. According to R. J. Stewart, author of *The Elements of Creation Myth*, the Indians of North America believed in a "cosmology which is basically shared, with variations, worldwide." The Aborigines of Australia refer to the beginning as the "Dreamtime." In *Primal Myths: Creating the World*, author Barbara C. Sproul writes that during the "Dreamtime" a wondrous, fertile being (three beings in one) from a realm of "not-being" wandered over the earth creating everything. As in most other myths, creation required a divine feminine participant. Most people today do not realize that even the Bible concurs, but the fact is, Genesis acknowledges a feminine component of the one God:

So God created man in *his own image*, in the image of God he created him; *male and female* he created them. (Genesis 1:27) [italics added]

The male/female nature of God is echoed in Genesis 5:1-2:

This is the book of the generations of Adam. When God created man, he made him in the likeness of God. Male and female he created them, and he blessed them and named them Man when they were created.

Despite the proliferation of gods and goddesses, divisions and personae, aspects and attributes that have been ascribed to deity, the similarities in these stories all lead us to a hint that a single intelligence created a single event that got the ball of creation rolling. As stated earlier, the Sufis accept oneness and insist that we have never been anything but one with God—and yet there is separation in our minds and hearts. A sense of separation in which we believe. From this point of departure, we will actually trace the fascinating story of oneness back through time to the beginning, when the "unfathomable totality"—the One— first moved. We will trace our oneness back to the center of the universe, and along the way we hope to reawaken to the Universal Consciousness within.

ONENESS IN ANCIENT SCRIPTURES

The abstinences (yamas) and observances (niyamas) are two of the eight limbs of yoga.* Whatever your chosen path back to oneness, let it be a reminder of the oneness of all holy scriptures, particularly to the Ten Commandments and to the teachings of Jesus.

The Abstinences

1. Nonviolence (causing of pain or death)
2. Nonlying (truthfulness)
3. Nonstealing (includes goods, ideas, honor, emotions)
4. Continence
5. Nongreed

The Observances

1. Purity
2. Contentment
3. Accepting but not causing pain
4. Study of spiritual books
5. Worship of God (self-surrender)

*The *Yoga Sutras of Patanjali* define the eight limbs of yoga as: the abstinences, observances, posture, breath control, sense withdrawal, concentration, meditation, and absorption into the superconscious (Universal Consciousness) state.

Chapter 3

I Am That I Am

IN THE NAME OF GOD

"The God of Genesis is a human creation, not the God at the center of the universe," writes Stephen Mitchell in his book *Genesis: A New Translation of the Classic Biblical Stories.* "Whenever God is presented as a character, that presentation is partial, therefore false. God is not a character in a story. God is the whole story."

The "unfathomable totality." The Ultimate Reality. The All. The One. Creator. Eternal, empty, and also completely full. God is all these things, because God is all things and God created all things. God has made this knowledge evident throughout history among every people in which the human heart has desired to know its connection to the divine. If we have lost this intimate connection with God, then we have only to seek it again in order to regain our sanity and our "divine intelligence" for living our lives to the fullest potential.

What better way to find oneness again than to retrace our "steps-in-consciousness" back to the beginning? Let this journey be an experience for your mind and heart, as we begin with the eternal soul that each of us possesses. The soul's immortality is described rather poetically in the Cayce readings:

Can God lose itself, if God be God—or is it submerged, or is it ... carried into the universal soul or consciousness? The *soul* is not lost; the *individuality* of the soul that separates itself is lost. (826-8)

The soul—the part of us that God created—can never be lost.

It is the deeply engaged *awareness* at the root of us, that never separated itself from oneness. As such, can that spark of awareness from the Creator actually forget its own origin?

Throughout our known history, there have been many auspicious and peculiar events in which God has tried to talk to us. God's name was revealed to Moses from the burning bush—I AM THAT I AM—and Moses was told to tell the children of Israel that I AM had sent him to them. What is this name and what does it mean? Obviously, I AM THAT I AM is not like a normal name. It is not a label name, such as Jack or Suzy, but it may be closer to a literal name, such as Sarah (from the Hebrew for "princess") or Peter (from the Greek for "rock"). It is a naked, plain, and simple declaration of pure Being.

Throughout the Bible, God is identified by various other names. Yahweh. The Lord. Most High God. Lord of Hosts. Elohim. *El* is an ancient Middle Eastern word for "deity" which found its way into various references to God (Isra*el*, Micha*el*, etc.). *El* is also related to the Arabic, *Allah*, in terms of its linguistic origins. However, in the Old Testament, particularly in Genesis, the plural form of this name is used: *El*ohim. This should not be surprising, for, as was pointed out in the previous chapter, God made humankind in "his" own image: "male and female." It is interesting to note that the "rib" reference in Genesis 2:21, when God created Eve, actually comes from a word meaning "side." Yet it wasn't the side of Adam's body being referred to, but his "feminine side," as in the feminine side of God's image.

God is also referred to as Yahweh, from the Hebrew letters YHWH, which mean I AM THAT I AM. (According to Huston Smith, "Jehovah" is an English misspelling of "Yahweh" that occurred during the King James translation.) Out of reverence, Jews use the address *Adonai* (Lord) instead of pronouncing the name *YHWH*, and in English-language bibles the name is often written simply as "Lord." But all of these references denote the ineffable name—I AM THAT I AM—that God spoke to Moses from the burning bush.

This holy name of God, macrocosm and microcosm all in one, echoes the mysterious names given to God in other religions, such as the Absolute or The Manifest and Unmanifest. I AM THAT I AM transcends all boundaries of perception—for it is everything. It is mystical, yet somehow so very intimate and personal. I AM is the simplemost declaration of consciousness itself.

I AM is all one—how can it be anything else, even if many beings are able to utter the name? *I AM is one.*

In discussions of oneness, the Edgar Cayce readings often refer to God's holy name, as well as to the I AM within each of us. The body, Cayce said, is "but the shadow or the temple of the living soul, or the real I AM that lives on and on." (633-2) As often occurred when people went to Edgar Cayce for a reading on some personal question, the reading would take the subject into the loftiest—or simplest, depending upon your point of view— truths in the universe. In 1936, a thirty-five-year-old lawyer was told:

God *is*, Spirit *is;* the Soul *is* an individualized portion that may materialize, that may become conscious as a companion for that which is, that I AM THAT I AM in *all* its spheres! And all spheres of activity in the earth, in the realms of *whatever* environ, are for that preparation. That man may control in the earth a few of its influences is so infinitesimal to what eternity is, or to what space or time or any of the universal forces are, that the finite mind does not conceive. (826-8)

Each one of us pronounces the name of God every time we refer to ourselves: "I am." I AM is the supreme declaration of Being, and, as the Cayce reading above points out, there is no end to I AM, not even in nature—there is only separation from it, which we ourselves have created through the rebellious, self-serving personality. Once $E=mc^2$ proved that matter and energy are one and the same, how are we to suppose that even the "very stones " (Luke 19:40) do not sing I AM THAT I AM? Science may yet catch up with spiritual wisdom on this point.

When God revealed God's holy name to Moses, it would really have taken the guesswork out of life for the Descendants of Abraham—if they had but perceived God simply and not created complications. God did not say to Moses, "I AM THAT I AM—but those words will have a different meaning when *you* say it!" The very name, whenever it is uttered, identifies the speaker with the name of God!

This is the I AM Father about which Christ said, "I and the Father are one." Christ, the Son of God, Emmanuel ("God with us") has been a part of ourselves from the very beginning, the perfect part of the soul that never forgets its oneness with God. This will be manifest when the whole world one day declares in unison, I AM THAT I AM, full aware of its meaning. Furthermore, no other name is needed for God or for our oneness with God:

> ...for names are setting metes and bounds—and to this edge and to that edge, which *does not* exist! any more than time, space or all—*when* you consider that the *soul* is *of* and *through* and part and portion of the all, see? (826-8)

I AM THAT I AM is known as "the Way" to the Taoists, as Nirvana to the Buddhists, and as *Brahma* (Creator) to the Hindus. But among many of the peoples who honor the ancient Vedas and chant their holy Sanskrit words, I AM THAT I AM is also known as the holy sound "Om." It is a symbol of the expression of spirit as love within the soul, the Logos, the Word. It is the simplest sound and name of the Allness of God declaring awareness of itself, just as we do (we who were created in the image of God) every time we say, "I am."

Swami Satchidananda, the founder of Integral Yoga International, gives an excellent description of Om. "Om is the sound of the Cosmic Vibration," he writes in *The Golden Present: Daily Inspirational Readings*. "The entire cosmos vibrates. Every cell vibrates. In fact, the whole universe is nothing but sound vibrations. The basic vibration is a hum, and the sum total of the universal vibration is also a hum. In between, there are fragments. All the words, all the languages, all the various sounds that are created by the human beings or animals or even machines are smaller parts of this cosmic hum. Without that hum, there is nothing. To denote that cosmic hum, there should be a word. Om is the word that comes closest to representing that cosmic hum. The word Om itself is not the hum. It's the name of the hum."

Om is known and used in all traditions that have come out of the ancient Vedic literature. The *Bhagavad Gita* (Chapter XVII) tells us, "'Om Tat Sat,' this is been considered to be the threefold designation of the Eternal. By that were ordained of old Brahmanas, Vedas and sacrifices. Therefore with the pronunciation of 'Om' the acts of sacrifice, gift and austerity as laid down in the ordinances are always commenced by the knowers of the Eternal."

Om is the sound that reverberates throughout the universe at all times. When we utter "I AM," we unite with this sound and we are one with it. When we pronounce Om, we are one with the sound of the eternal utterance of God, I AM THAT I AM.

THE PATRIARCHS IN EGYPT

Throughout human history, God has reached through the veil of our forgetfulness many times to awaken us—our Creator's sleeping children who chose to separate themselves from Universal Consciousness. Communications from the Most High, through prophets, for example, have accompanied all the steps humankind has taken since the creation of Adam. They often occurred in the form of agreements, or covenants, in which God made promises of beauty, protection, progeny, and salvation in exchange for the people agreeing not to forget who God is by obeying the laws and by practicing love.

God promised eternal life to Adam and Eve if they would not eat of the tree of the knowledge of good and evil. That covenant broken, humankind proceeded onward until: "The LORD saw that the wickedness of man was great in the earth, and that every imagination of the thoughts of his heart was only evil continually" (Genesis 6:5), and God had to destroy the world with a great flood. Humankind and animal life were saved—two by two in the ark. Then God made a new covenant with Noah, and with all life, never to destroy the world again by flood. God would put a "bow in the clouds" to symbolize the new covenant.

Next, with a man named Abram of Ur, God got more specific. God promised the aged and childless Abram that he would become a "great nation." If Abram would worship the one God, Abram would have descendants as many as the stars and would lead them into the land of milk and honey—Canaan, the Promised Land—that would be theirs forevermore. This covenant was sealed by changing Abram's name to Abraham and by promising to identify the Chosen People by circumcising the males thereafter—an unmistakable reminder in anyone's book. After a sojourn in Egypt, which is described in Genesis 12:10, Ishmael was born to Abraham with the servant Haggar, and Isaac was eventually born to Abraham with his wife Sarah. Thus commenced the generations which would become Israel, out of which would come the Messiah.

God reached out once again to Isaac with the promise of "an everlasting covenant" and again to his son Jacob, whom He renamed "Israel"—covenants designed to keep the children of Israel forever mindful of God's oneness. This was difficult to do in a world full of warring tribes and seductive cults. But Israel fared well in Canaan, even when Joseph's brothers sold him and convinced Jacob that Joseph had been killed. However, Joseph, too, ended up in Egypt, where he matured and, because of his ability to interpret dreams, was eventually put in charge of Egypt's lands in order to prepare for a terrible famine that Joseph had foreseen. The famine came and spread as far as Canaan, where Joseph's treacherous brothers heard that Egypt's cities had put up plenty of extra grain.

Joseph eventually forgave his brothers. In fact, his statement in Genesis 50:20 is considered by many scholars to be an interpretive key to the entire Old Testament: "As for you," said Joseph to his brothers, "you meant evil against me; but God meant it for good . . . " Later, Pharaoh invited Jacob to Egypt, and he journeyed from Canaan with seventy members of Israel to meet Joseph. Israel dwelled, then, in Egypt as guests for many generations. Eventually, Jacob passed on and so did Joseph, but not long after Joseph's death the Egyptians declared the Israelites slaves. Three hundred and fifty years of slavery and subjugation later, however, we encounter Moses, and I AM THAT I AM. We return to Moses, because shortly after Moses was born, a Pharaoh who "knew not Joseph" decided to wipe the Israelites out by slaying all their male children.

Pharaoh's edict that the sons of Israel should be killed prompted Moses' mother, Jochebed, to fear for his life. So unfolds the story of how she placed him in a basket and how one of Pharaoh's daughters found him. She paid Jochebed to nurse him, but then secretly raised him as her own. It is interesting to note that, like Abraham, Joseph, and Jacob, Moses spent considerable time in Egypt.

In order to lead the Israelites out of Egypt, in about 1250 B.C., I AM THAT I AM gave Moses the power to perform miracles. He would lead the Israelites back home to the Promised Land and leave the Egyptian army treading water in the Red Sea. Along the way, however, the Israelites became forgetful. Moses heard I AM THAT I AM speak, and eventually God made a new covenant with the Israelites in the form of the Ten Commandments. God made other covenants later—for example, with Solomon, David, and Jesus—but with the Egyptian connection in mind, our tracing of the story of oneness and God's name now takes an unexpected turn.

Scholars and theologians differ on the effects that Egyptian

language and theology may have had on the Israelites, but the
Descendants of Abraham must recognize that four of its great
patriarchs—Abraham, Jacob, Joseph, and Moses—lived in Egypt
for many years and must have been influenced by the ideas they
encountered there. While the Descendants of Abraham tend to
look no further than holy scripture for the roots of I AM THAT I
AM, the Edgar Cayce readings provide compelling insights into
these influences. For example, the Bible, along with the readings,
tells us that Moses himself received certain ancient teachings
while he was growing up. The book of Acts states, "And Moses
was instructed in all the wisdom of the Egyptians, and he was
mighty in his words and deeds." (Acts 7:22) The readings tell us
that Moses was reared

**. . . as not merely an Egyptian but from the associations with
Jochebed [Moses' mother] the entity learned from the scribe
Ezekiai (?) of those promises that had been made to the saints
before Abraham, Isaac and Jacob. (2574-1) [italics added]**

The readings do not specify what these "promises" were, however. German mystic, Rudolf Steiner, maintained from his own
psychic sources that Moses received training in Egypt; furthermore, that he received it in the Great Pyramid, which was not a
tomb at all. Now, however, we are compelled to pick up the
golden thread of oneness in Egypt, a century before Moses lived.

THE BOOK OF THE LIVING

The world's great religious ideas seem to have sprung from
the same source, beginning with simple ideas divinely designed
to show the people the way back to oneness. Once humans decided to administrate and interpret the ideas, however, it was
only a matter of time before the simple became complicated,
eventually requiring reformers in order to help the faithful get
back on track.

The story of the Descendants of Abraham is a continuing
struggle against idolatry, as is the story of the early Christians
and of most other religions, too. Some Christians, after all, believe that the Bible tells them that they must handle poisonous
snakes in order to prove their faith. Could the original writers of
the Upanishads really have had a cruel caste system in mind for
India? Did Muhammad intend that Islam should split in two, and
that his Sunni followers should one day make war with his Shiite

followers? With the same questions applied to ancient Egypt, was
the Egyptian pantheon of jackals, hawks, and ibises actually a
set of divine symbols that had run amuck due to dynastic amne-
sia of the original idea? Were those "gods" merely like the Hindu
gods—just aspects of the one true God? As with the interpreters
of other scriptures, is it possible that the modern interpreters of
hieroglyphics have merely been too literal?

History shows that a religion, pure as it may have been in its
beginnings, eventually falls victim to additions, subtractions,
and other corruptions, requiring a saint to set it right again.
Strangely, one can see a pattern of 1,500 years in many religions—between the inception and the need for reform. Christianity entered a reformation led by Martin Luther around A.D.
1500. By A.D. 1000, Buddhism (begun around 500 B.C.) needed
Padma Sambhava to reinstate Buddha's original intent. With this
oddly coincidental 1,500-year breaking point, we may look to Islam (begun around A.D. 500) for reforms in progress now or to
come, of which the current swing toward fundamentalism may
be a part. Interestingly, it seems that ancient Egypt was no ex-
ception to this 1,500-year pattern.

Dynastic Egypt began around 3100 B.C., when King Menes of
the South conquered the North and made the "two lands" of
Egypt one nation. But roughly 1,500 years after Menes, around
1360 B.C., a king named Amenhotep IV set about, with furious
determination, to reform Egyptian religion in a way that was
most peculiar to the Egyptians of his day. Moses wouldn't live for
another 100 years, but there are two fascinating connections between the two of them.

The Cayce readings state that before God said to Moses I AM
THAT I AM, Moses had received training in mysteries that pre-
dated Abraham (Abraham lived about a thousand years before
Moses). Knowing as we do that God has existed always, we
would look for signs of divine intervention in human history
prior to Abraham, for some clue that I AM and oneness were
known or at least available in scriptures. But Egyptian records
tell us little about history before the First Dynasty. Various
Bronze Age tribes, the experts say, had come and gone, but there
is little archaeological or anthropological evidence to suggest
that a more sophisticated culture existed then.

In the 1890s, E. A. Wallis Budge, of the British Museum, began
to publish translations of the *Egyptian Book of the Dead*. This

ancient work, considered to be one of the world's finest art trea-
sures, is a collection of 100 smaller texts from different periods
that had been gathered from various tombs by the Egyptians and
copied during the Eighteenth and Nineteenth Dynasties (1570
B.C.-1200 B.C.) for inclusion in their tombs. Budge himself noted
that the title of the book was a misnomer, having been carried
over from early grave robbers who simply referred to the texts as
"a book stolen from a dead man." He also mentioned that many
of the texts were far older, dating back to pre-Dynastic times and
possibly as far back as 5000 B.C. or earlier. The Edgar Cayce readings confirm that the *Egyptian Book of the Dead* is much older
than scholars realize, and also that:

> **. . . the Book of the Dead, as it was called in the present . . .
> was rather the Book of Life; or it represents that which is** *the*
> *experience of a soul* **in its sojourn not only in the land of Nir-
> vana (?), the land of Nod, or the land of night, but rather those
> things that make for the cleansing of a physical body for the
> aptitudes of expression . . . to the spiritual truths. (706-1)** [ital-
> ics added]

The *Book of the Dead*, according to Cayce, is a book of spiritual teachings, not merely a guide for mummified dignitaries. In
Budge's translation of "The Elysian Fields" (*Book of the Dead*,
Chapter CX), we find the following, "For behold, I repose at the
seasons [of Horus]. I have passed through the region of the company of the gods who are aged and venerable." However, this
same passage, in another translation (Blackden), reads as fol-
lows:

> **For "I am" is my rest in His seasons; even He who when He
> manifests His plan, the Company of the Gods becomes His first-
> born children.**

Through Budge, we receive one of the most startling esoteric
insights pertaining to the Egyptian religious system—that, indeed, modern interpreters of the hieroglyphic records have overlooked the truth of oneness to be found there. In 1839, a
researcher named Champollion-Fegeac wrote:

> **The Egyptian religion is a pure monotheism, which mani-
> fested itself externally by a symbolic polytheism. (***The Egyptian
> Book of the Dead***, University Books edition, 1966, p. 106)**

According to Budge, the Egyptians were copying these already
ancient texts and placing them in tombs between 1500 B.C. and
900 B.C. Since Moses worked directly for the Pharaoh and led

the Israelites out of Egypt around 1250 B.C., it is tempting to point out that Moses may well have been exposed to the ideas expressed in the *Book of the Dead*. This would not imply that he did not hear the name I AM THAT I AM spoken from the burning bush, but perhaps such previous exposure helped him to understand what God would be trying to tell him on Mt. Sinai. Whether or not he was exposed to the *Egyptian Book of the Dead* is unknown, although hints from Luke (Acts 7:22), Edgar Cayce, and Rudolf Steiner provide a foundation for speculation.

This brings us to another intriguing Egyptian connection that will help us in our journey. This connection can be found in the story of one of history's strangest heretics.

THE VOICE AKHENATEN HEARD

"The further back in time we glimpse our ancestors, the more like ourselves they become," writes Donald B. Redford in his seminal work, *Akhenaten: The Heretic King*. But could this possibly be true for a deformed, misshapen heretic who, during his reign, would order Egyptians to jettison their gods, and afterward be called *The Enemy?*

At various times in Egyptian history, the geographical centers of political influence changed, and each one enjoyed a popularity by turn, establishing systems of thought and individual families of gods. Chiefly, these centers were at Memphis (the cult of Ptah), Hermopolis (the cult of Thoth), and Heliopolis (the Sun cult of Re or Ra). Setting aside the idolatrous aspects of the cults that evolved there, a fascinating connection links them together.

As Redford explains, the Egyptians "strongly tended toward explaining the apparent plurality of the cosmos in terms of an underlying unity." The Memphite system of cosmology (the cult of Ptah) praised Heart (defined as Mind) as the primal element. "Heart," he writes, "had given existence to things by thinking, by concrete projection of willed thought." That is to say, everything exists because of the underlying unity, namely Heart. The second system is associated with Hermopolis (the cult of Thoth), and it identified a common oneness, naming it the "Infinite." But most interestingly, Redford explains that the third, the Heliopolitan system (having had the most ancient temples of all), embraced Atum, the "All-Inclusive," the "One," from whom all entities came.

When the odd-looking and deformed Amenhotep IV (1380-1362 B.C.) came into power, Amun (the sun god "whose body is unknown; in whom are all gods") was the god of choice. Redford observes that by that time, the Amun temples had become rife with nepotism, corruption, and internal power struggles. Amun was known as the "living torch which emerged from the flood," an obvious connection to the Noah story and one which is repeated in mythologies around the world. To Amun is attributed the creation of all life, the "tree of life" (perhaps the Egyptian predecessor to the kabbalistic Tree of Life), including the earth and humankind.

There were sun gods in all of the Egyptian cults. Jeremy Naydler, author of *Temple of the Cosmos*, says, "More than any other cosmic body, the sun was, for the Egyptians, an image of the concentrated power of the heavenly realm." Although various attributes were ascribed to each, Naydler sees in the interpretation not a literal worshiping of the sun, but a worshiping of the divine power that it *symbolized* for them, in the sun.

Records show that Amenhotep IV claimed that the Sun-god itself (a sun-god form called Re-Harakhty) told him to order the country to worship only one God, now translated as "the great living sun disc." In the fifth year of his reign, he ordered old temples closed, new temples built, and hieroglyphic records covered over with plaster so that the name of Amun would be replaced by that of Aten, the new name for the One God. The king then changed his own name from Amenhotep IV (the Divine, the Ruler of Thebes) to Akhenaten (Glorified Spirit of the Sun-disc).

The changes Akhenaten wrought were immediate and sweeping. He moved the palace, appointed all new administrators, and changed the style of art. During his reign, Egypt lost most of her holdings in Asia. Ultimately, the people despised him, hence the name *The Enemy*, which was applied to him for generations. The people soon went back to their polytheistic ways, and historians now doubt that Akhenaten's philosophy had much lasting effect on the Egyptian people. But it is highly possible that Akhenaten's ideas influenced the patriarchs of the Old Testament or, at least, were part of a divine wake-up call that was reborn in the bosom of Abraham.

Egyptian theology, in its simplemost, original idea, acknowledged oneness at the root of all that exists. Akhenaten actually tried to establish the one God in the minds of the people. He, too, may well have been trying to implement the spiritual truths of the *Book of the Dead.* Whatever the case, it is interesting to note that Akhenaten's grandfather, Thutmose IV, had once erected a single obelisk at Karnak dedicated to Re-Harakhty (Aten).

Perhaps it is not unreasonable to wonder if God tried to reach out with the message of oneness to a sleeping humanity even through these ancient Egyptian rulers. But a number of intriguing questions arise: Is it possible that Moses knew the *Book of the Dead?* Even though Egyptian records make no mention even of the existence of the Hebrew patriarchs, is it even possible that ideas from Abraham could have influenced Akhenaten some 900 years later? Or could it be, despite how Akhenaten's people hated his "One God" idea, that God had tried to speak to Akhenaten in the same way in which God had successfully spoken to Moses?

It may not be possible to answer these questions, but the golden thread remains in our grasp, leading us, as we shall see, even deeper into Egypt's past.

The following passage is the opening stanza of a hymn to Aten attributed to Akhenaten's time, and it further illustrates possible Egyptian influences in the traditions of the Descendants of Abraham. The translation is by Neil Douglas-Klotz from his book, *Desert Wisdom,* in which he refers to Aten as "Aton as the Sun." Interestingly, the hymn sings the praises of the one God with reference to a trinity:

> *Praise to the Three-in-One of the Sun:*
> *Praise to* Re, *the Streak of light we see.*
> *Praise to* Har-akhti, *who appears pregnant at dawn.*
> *Praise to* Shu, *who maintains a balance of heat and power.*
> *All live eternally in the disk of Aton—*
> *the ultimate Thou-and-I in all beings,*
> *our Mutual Soul.*

DOORS TO THE PAST

Clearly, the idea of oneness actually predates dynastic Egypt, disappearing, as though unrecorded, into the mists of history. But there is a record from which we can continue to follow the golden thread of oneness—and remember oneness within ourselves. That record is in the Edgar Cayce readings, which describe an advanced civilization that thrived there around 10,500 B.C. The readings say, in fact, that it was at the end of this lost civilization, not during the Fourth Dynasty period of Chephren (2500 B.C.), that built the Great Pyramid and the Great Sphinx. As early as 1928, certain readings had begun to refer to "the people, in the land now known as Egypt, and the time 10,500 years before the Prince of Peace came . . . " (105-2)

On July 1, 1932, a group of people in Norfolk, Virginia, who had received readings from Cayce, gathered in order to receive more detailed information. They were called the Norfolk Study Group No. 1, and together they studied the growing volume of Cayce's marvelous readings. That day they asked the following questions of Cayce:

(Q) What was the date of the actual beginning and ending of the construction of the Great Pyramid?

(A) Was one hundred years in construction. Begun and completed in the period of Araaraart's time, with Hermes and Ra.

(Q) What was the date B.C. of that period?

(A) 10,490 to 10,390 before the Prince entered into Egypt. (5748-6)

We will examine the story of this civilization and the mysterious individuals, Araaraart, Hermes, and Ra, in the next chapter. In the meantime, however, we must deal with the fact that conventional Egyptologists attribute the Great Pyramid and Sphinx at Gizeh to Chephren and have been satisfied with that dating for many years.

Cayce's supposition presents a problem of credibility. After all, in his readings, he described the life, the politics, the spirituality, the romance, and the intrigue of the various people who inhabited Egypt at that time. Since Cayce is the most well-documented psychic on record, his amazing readings on prehistory cannot be dismissed out of hand. They are especially vital in our quest to rediscover our oneness and remember our place in Universal Consciousness.

Even though most Egyptologists still adhere to the Fourth Dynasty dating of the Gizeh necropolis, there are at least two scientists who have recently offered compelling evidence that the Great Pyramid and the Great Sphinx, unlike the other tombs and monuments on the same plateau, are actually much older.

In October 1991, geologist Robert M. Schoch, a Yale graduate and associate professor at Boston University, presented a paper to the Geological Society of America challenging the accepted age of the Great Sphinx. He is among the first scientists to roll back the probable age of the Sphinx, stating that its initial carving must have occurred as early as 5000 to 7000 B.C.

What convinced the geologist was his discovery that the Great Sphinx exhibits a different erosion pattern than the other structures on the plateau, which have suffered chiefly from wind erosion. The limestone in the Sphinx, he said, is eroded from precipitation, enough precipitation to create a "rolling, undulating" surface—and there hasn't been that kind of precipitation in the area since 5000 B.C. and before. Schoch's paper details other reasons why he believes the Great Sphinx to be older. Although he does not exclude the possibility that the Sphinx may be as old as Cayce said it is, he has not yet found the required evidence. But there is even more convincing evidence that Cayce was right. In this case, from the stars.

In their book, *The Orion Mystery*, authors Robert Bauval and Adrian Gilbert set out to prove that the Great Pyramid and its neighbor monuments are not tombs at all, but rather parts of an ancient time-marking system. They offer powerful evidence, through astronomical calculations, that the floor plan of the Gizeh pyramids actually marks the exact pattern of the stars in the constellation Orion, specifically, the three-star belt. Do the pyramids point at these stars now? No. But *The Orion Mystery* authors used sophisticated calculations to "turn back" the stars to their positions when the pyramids were built.

What they were trying to do was to pinpoint the "First Time of Osiris"—the Lord of all things—the beginning point of the Egyptian cosmology, and they hoped that the star positions would show it to them. The evidence is both controversial and convincing, especially in light of Cayce readings. Their conclusion is that the Great Pyramid was built when their positions marked exactly the positions of the stars in Orion—10,450 B.C.

Author and researcher Graham Hancock offers a voluminous list of evidence that the planetary, climactic, and social history of our world is quite different from what has traditionally been thought. In his thoroughly researched book, *Fingerprints of the Gods*, he examines various ancient chronologies, such as the Palermo Stone, Manetho, and the Turin Papyrus, which, he says, "agree on a very ancient date for the First Time of Osiris: the golden age when the gods were believed to have ruled in Egypt.

In addition, the sources demonstrate a striking convergence over the importance they accord to the eleventh millennium B.C. in particular . . . " He also cites evidence of an as-yet-unexplained "agricultural revolution"—the earliest anywhere in the world.

Of course, none of these recent scientific discoveries proves that Edgar Cayce was correct. However, they lend enough support to persuade skeptics and believers alike to lend an ear to the extraordinary Egyptian story that is told in the Cayce readings. Though speculation is interesting, what is more exciting is the prospect of discovering that the oneness of God, and perhaps even God's holy name, I AM THAT I AM, has been known to humankind even in prehistory. As scientists begin to nod at prehistoric evidence, we can continue the search for our innate knowledge of oneness in the psychic records of Edgar Cayce, where our journey will take us beyond the Egyptians, even to the beginning of time itself.

ONE SOUL, MANY COSTUMES

In order to proceed, it is important to introduce the subject of the returning soul—reincarnation. This is because, when we journey back in time, understanding the cyclic return of souls as individuals and groups becomes important. Yes, say the Cayce readings, our souls existed from the beginning. Yes, we have returned many times throughout history. We were the creators of our history. We are the captains of our fate, in very many ways.

After he had finished giving a reading, Edgar Cayce would often awaken and be amazed at the material that had come through him. One such time occurred in 1923, when a prosperous Ohio businessman named Arthur Lammers received in his first reading (5717-1) information that he "was once a monk" in another life. Cayce's first reference to reincarnation can be found in reading 4841-1, given April 22, 1911. However, the former reading identifies, for the first time, the nature of the individual's past life.

The contribution that the Cayce readings have made to a Western understanding of reincarnation is well known. As souls, say the readings, we have many chances to learn our lessons in the schoolroom of the earth, not just one. Our bodies, therefore, are projections of our souls through parent-hosts into the three-dimensional plane. When the body dies, we withdraw back into the nonphysical planes and, whether out of necessity or desire, return through new parents in a new body.

Beyond revealing that the soul lives in a succession of bodies, instead of just one, Mr. Lammers's reading led to an intensive series of questions that pertained to past lives. As was stated in chapter 1, Cayce had been a conservative Christian. When he learned that "past-life" information had come through, he became upset and began to doubt the source of the readings. In a subsequent reading done on himself, however, he was advised to re-read the Bible from the point of view of reincarnation, which he did. The exercise opened a whole new understanding of the Bible for Cayce, helping to convince him of the validity of the idea of the returning soul.

In the thousands of readings that followed, Cayce conveyed information that peered into every period of recorded and unrecorded history—revealing previously unknown details about the workings of the continuing soul, our origins, and our connection to God.

One of the most amazing series of readings that Cayce gave were the life readings. These 1,919 readings contain the comprehensive histories of individual souls, about their spiritual, mental, and physical makeup—as well as detailed information about the individual's past incarnations.

How does the idea of reincarnation tie in to the theme of oneness? The fact is, a returning soul, as opposed to a soul who receives "one chance" at life, fills out our understanding of oneness in a most satisfying way. The reason for this is that, as we were not always separate from oneness, we are neither separate from our problems and failings, nor from our talents and blessings. They are not simply bestowed for one time use, but earned by us in successions of embodiments in the earth. Even though "we" as a race descended into the material, the soul between incarnations is still magnetized to the earth through its desires and through its need for continued learning. That which is built in the physical plane must be overcome in the material plane.

Cayce had much to say about reincarnation. He was even asked to respond to a question about arguments against it. His answer, however, explains that even though we are individuals, the purpose is for us to realize our oneness with God through soul growth:

But the strongest argument against reincarnation is also,

turned over, the strongest argument for it ... For the *law* is set—and it happens! though a soul may will itself *never* to reincarnate, but must burn and burn and burn—or suffer and suffer and suffer! For, the heaven and hell is built by the soul! The companionship in God is being one with Him; and the gift of God is being conscious of being one with Him, yet apart from Him—or one with, yet apart from, the Whole. (5753-1)

The Cayce readings state that reincarnation is necessary because our desires and errors have made it so. Reincarnation provides us with the opportunities by which we can grow into the perfection of the Universal Consciousness and regain our oneness. We are not the disconnected pawns of fickle fate nor are we victimized by the inequalities of our stations at birth. We operate in life according to universal laws, one of which is the Law of Cause and Effect, known in the East as *karma*, which works hand-in-hand with reincarnation. In its essence, karma dictates that "whatever a man sows, that he will also reap." (Galatians 6:7) The law applies whether in the material, mental, or spiritual activities.

"Destiny is within," says reading 903-23, "or is as ... the gift of the Creative Forces. Karmic influence is, then, rebellious influence against such ... Then in *every* contact is there the opportunity for an entity ... to embrace that necessary for the entity to enter into the at-oneness with that Creative Force."

Among the life readings are the 294 series, which contains the readings Edgar Cayce gave on the history of his own soul. These readings reveal a fascinating array of details from many historical periods. One of the most interesting is the story of an advanced civilization that Cayce said existed in Egypt around 10,500 B.C., our next stop along the golden thread of oneness. Whether the reader is prepared to accept the idea of many incarnations, rather than only a single life, the material in the life readings covers fascinating, unknown periods in human prehistory. Our ultimate destination of oneness is well worth the trip.

THE TEN COMMANDMENTS OF
I Am That I Am

Exodus 20:3-17

Meditate upon the Ten Commandments using insights from the Edgar Cayce readings to gain a deeper understanding of their vital importance in your rediscovering your oneness.

1. You shall have no other gods before me.
    > For he that putteth position, self, power, money, place, before the God—*that* becomes the god, and must crumble before the Throne! (257-36)

2. You shall not make for yourself a graven image, or any likeness of anything that is in heaven above, or that is in the earth beneath, or that is in the water under the earth . . .
    > Keep thyself in that way and *manner* as is acceptable to Him, the Giver of all good and perfect gifts—and keep thyself from idols. (254-34)

3. You shall not take the name of the Lord your God in vain; for the Lord will not hold him guiltless who takes his name in vain.
    > For, He is humble—yet the Lord of all; gracious, yet to Him all power is given; loving, yet to him do those in distress and in power use oft His name in vain. Let Him come and abide with thee. Open thine heart, thine soul, to His ways. (378-45)

4. Remember the sabbath day, to keep it holy . . .
    > For the day itself is as nothing. Remember how He as the Teacher of teachers gave that the Sabbath was made for man, *not* man for the Sabbath! (3976-21)

5. Honor your father and your mother, that your days may be long in the land which the Lord your God gives you.
    > What meanest this? Only as each soul becomes as the father, the mother, is it aware of the meaning. (254-111)

6. You shall not kill.

. . . thoughts are deeds, and may become crimes or miracles. (900-201)

7. You shall not commit adultery.
    As has been indicated in that "Whom the Lord loveth He chasteneth," and purgeth every one; for corruption may *not* inherit eternal life, and must be burned up. (262-26)

8. You shall not steal.
    Be rather "done" by all, than ever taking advantage of *any* individual! For he that overcometh shall wear the crown, and not he that climbeth up some other way—for he becomes the thief, the robber to self . . . (1792-2)

9. You shall not bear false witness against your neighbor.
    As given, let all be done in meekness, in sincerity and in truth. *Never* present that as an untruth to force an issue with the developing mind. (324-5)

10. You shall not covet your neighbor's house; you shall not covet your neighbor's wife . . . or anything that is your neighbor's.
    For hate and jealousy are no easier to be seen or felt than mercy and love. (1066-1)

Chapter 4

THE LAW OF ONE

RA TA

One of the most irresistible accounts in the Edgar Cayce readings is that of Ra Ta—the priestly reformer who was the first to manifest the spirit of Ra in Egypt.

The history of Ra Ta came about in the readings, initially, by questioners who asked Cayce how he acquired his wonderful psychic gifts. The answer was that he had possessed them, in part, because of his experiences in past lives. One of these past lives was as Ra Ta, "son of a daughter of Zu" (294-147), in the region of Mt. Ararat.

Apparently, Akhenaten wasn't the only strange-looking leader to have lived in ancient Egypt, because Ra Ta, too, would have appeared strange to the people of his time. He was "Six feet one-inch tall, weighing . . . a hundred and eighty-one pounds. Fair of face, not too much hair on the head nor too much on the face or body. In color nearly white, only sun or air tanned." (275-38) His blond hair and blue eyes added to the effect amid the Middle Eastern community in which he lived.

His appearance created condemnation among his people, but Ra Ta had been born with a deep spiritual awareness and acute intuitive gifts. He had the gift of prophecy and was able to see into the future. Once his gifts were recognized by King Ararat, he designated Ra Ta a priest and began to rely on him for guidance. One of Ra Ta's prophecies was that he and the king's son, Arart, would invade Egypt and take it over in order to establish "that *principle* [which] became the basis for the studies of the Prince of Peace, and the establishing *of* those schools as began in the land by those that overran the land." (1734-3)

The Prince of Peace? Jesus had said, "before Abraham was, I am." (John 8:58) But no one would deny that references to the Messiah are unheard of in the scant archaeological records available from that time. Yet, this reference to Ra Ta indicates a mysterious link to Christ, from a time nearly 6,000 years before Abraham. It was a teaching that heralded the arrival of the Messiah, 10,500 years hence! With all of the evidence that supports the accuracy of Cayce's other readings and the undoubtable devotion he held in his life to the Bible and to the Master, this psychic record is compelling indeed.

Ra Ta, at twenty-one years of age, along with Arart and a force of 900 invaded Egypt, then under the rule of a complacent and weary King Raai. Once the natives learned the invaders' intent to establish temples, conduct training, and inspire them with spiritual teachings, they yielded with very little fighting.

The Egypt that Ra Ta and Arart invaded is described in the readings as a country which already had:

. . . those things that are classed in the present as pleasures that gratify the senses of man's own development, for much that is now as the developments that are necessities as well as luxuries were *then* commonplace as the most common necessities in the present. (294-147)

In this land, this reading states, Ra Ta eventually established "easy, even control of a land that might be said to be supplying then all the luxuries of the earth in that particular period." (294-147)

The natives of Egypt willingly participated, at least for a while, in Ra Ta's reforms, which established a religion built on the idea of the one God. For the serious flaws that then existed in the people—in both demeanor, desire, and the physical body—he built temples in which the people were alchemically cleansed, in body, mind, and spirit, for greater service to God. These temples were called the Temple of Sacrifice and the Temple Beautiful.

The following reading describes some details on what occurred in those temples:

As to the manner of the service there: The individuals having cleansed themselves of those appendages that hindered, came not merely for the symbolic understanding. For these, to be sure, were all symbolized . . . in the light or the lamp borne by

those who served as the Light Bearers to those who entered for their initiation, or for their preparation to be that as given by the teachers—even *Ra Ta.*

Laying aside those things that easily beset the sons of men, ye as ye enter here, put thy whole trust in the one God, that ye may be all things unto all men, thereby crucifying thine own desires that they—thy brethren—may know the Lord their God. (281-25)

Edgar Cayce's soul-memory of his life as Ra Ta is full of intrigue, treachery, banishment, and triumph; however, it is a key step along the golden thread by which we can trace oneness and fully understand how our separation from God occurred.

We begin with the readings' references to the priest Ra Ta's own practice of archaeology with the natives in Egypt, wherein he began "uncovering the records" and earning much credibility. This was because the records revealed proof of what the priest had been teaching. It was through the priest, the readings say, that the Great Pyramid and the Great Sphinx were built, by Arart, his son Araaraart, and the architect Hermes (called Trismegistus or "thrice great" in the early centuries A.D.). Hermes was one of the incarnations of Jesus, according to the readings. (See "Enoch, Hermes, and Melchizedek" in chapter 5.) Reading 5748-5 states that the Great Sphinx was built "some 10,500 [years] before the coming of the Christ into the land . . . "

Our golden thread reveals that Ra Ta had been born for a preplanned purpose. The readings recall the period just prior to his birth and shows how his soul chose the time, the mother, and the people among whom to be born. With the work Ra Ta would do in Egypt as its goal, his soul foresaw that the son of Ararat would conquer Egypt. His soul knew that this would provide him the best opportunity to give "the entrance into the Holy of Holies," to give "the rule to [the] people" (341-9), and to establish a temple for worshiping the Most High God.

THE HALL OF RECORDS

Can we assume that Ra Ta had, by divine order or otherwise, simply chosen without any previous cause to be born in order to steer an indifferent humanity toward God? The readings are very clear that this is not the case. For an answer, we look at the "Hall of Records," for it will help us discover a host of other civilizations that existed even before the time of Ra Ta.

The readings tell us a great deal about the "Hall of Records," a chamber that was hidden by Ra Ta, Araaraart (Arart's son), and Hermes, near the right paw of the Sphinx. Cayce said that the chamber contains ancient records about the history of the human race and spoke about a legendary lost continent called Atlantis. As we are about to learn, however, Atlantis was not merely a legend, but fact. Moreover, we were all there in other bodies, living and working together in some ways like we are now.

According to the readings, the Hall of Records is a secret chamber—a sealed room—in which records of the "true teaching," as the Atlantean priests had taught it, were stashed by Ra Ta and his associates.

(Q) Give in detail what the sealed room contains.

(A) A record of Atlantis from the beginnings of those periods when the Spirit took form or began the encasements [incarnations] in that land, and the developments of the peoples throughout their sojourn, with the record of the first destruction and the changes that took place in the land . . . and the buildings of the pyramid of initiation, with who, what, where, would come the opening of the records that are as copies from the sunken Atlantis; for with the change it must rise (the temple) again. (378-16)

These, then, would be the records by which the world would find its intimate roots in the one, in the I AM presence—oneness with God. Many people actively seek to discover the records of which Cayce spoke, but they have not been found. There are many readings about this period of Ra Ta and the records of Atlantis, which played a vital role in preparing for the Messiah and continues to play a role in the Second Coming. This is because the readings pinpoint when the Hall of Records will be found—*and it is in our own time:*

For, these [records] were to be kept as had been given by the priests in Atlantis or Poseidia (Temple), when these records of the race, of the developments, of the laws pertaining to One were put in their chambers and to be opened only when there was the returning of those into materiality, or to earth's experience, when the change was imminent in the earth; which change, we see, begins in '58 and ends with the changes wrought in the upheavals and the shifting of the poles, as be-

gins then the reign in '98 ... (378-16)

Predictions of dour events for the end of our century notwithstanding, the legacy of Ra Ta in the land of Egypt was manifold as his activities helped to usher in a new era in human evolution. But why was it necessary to hide the records? What had happened before this time that made the appearance of Ra Ta so important for the future of humankind? What happened to the Atlantean people, and why was it necessary to keep the records a secret for so long? The answer to this question can be found in how and why we *separated from oneness*.

LOST CONTINENTS

The Cayce readings make it clear that the reason we have forgotten our oneness is directly related to our choice to separate from God and from each other—the very points, as we discovered in chapter 2, that Jesus stated were the first and second greatest commandments. (Mark 12:29-31) The truth is that, deep within our souls, we have never completely lost our connection to oneness; we have merely let our higher senses atrophy from disuse and allowed ourselves to believe that we must remain separate. What occurred in Atlantis was the spiritual linchpin by which we lost "oneness" as our way of life, thinking, creating, and being.

In 1954, author and historian, L. Sprague de Camp, published his book *Lost Continents: The Atlantis Theme in History, Science, and Literature*. Up until that time, scores of writers had published various accounts and interpretations of lost continents from the points of view of history, philosophy, and occultism. However, it was de Camp's stated purpose in writing the book to separate "fact from fiction," and insofar as scientific fact was understood in the mid-twentieth century, his book remains a useful directory of the then-known writing on the subject.

Along the way, de Camp looks only disinterestedly at the psychic records of occultists such as Rudolf Steiner and Mme. Helene Blavatsky, whose Theosophical material, he implied, was derived from the work of other writers. Edgar Cayce, mentioned only once, is dismissed as a "hillbilly clairvoyant-diagnostician." Even so, de Camp favors writers such as the Scottish mythologist Lewis Spence, who was a contemporary of Cayce and hesitant to stray from prevailing scientific thought. His book, *History of*

Atlantis, was first published in 1924, a year after Cayce first began giving readings on Atlantis.

Spence's book offered sound evidence that supported some of Cayce's Atlantis information. For example, it affirms Cayce's hypothesis that a continent did exist in the mid-Atlantic Ocean, that it was destroyed over time through geologic catastrophe, that it suffered a disaster around 25,000 B.C., and finally disappeared around 10,000 B.C.

L. Sprague de Camp also examined the writings of Paul Schliemann, Ignatius Donnelly, and James Churchward, dismissing them as "pseudo-scientists," and perhaps rightly so, at least in regard to their unsupported conclusions. However, de Camp overlooks the big picture, ignoring the commonalities of independent intuitive sources and placing as much faith in the ever-shifting sands of science just as Plato did in his day. He concludes: "I hope that I have shown that the arguments of most members of the Atlantis cult are not to be taken very seriously."

Yet, the fact that hundreds of writers and thinkers throughout the ages have bound themselves to the topic tells us something significant. It tells us that we are seeking in the outside world the heartfelt knowing among all people that we all need and feel love. We are homesick for a union, deep in our memory, history, and divinity, of knowing God on a first-name basis. Having oneness with perfection in a utopian universe. Living without terror and without error. We long for perfect happiness as though we remember having it before. The metaphor of the Garden of Eden begins to take on form and character, especially when we view it with a complete history of our presence on earth.

Science may yet incorporate intuitive knowledge in its *what-you-see-is-what-you-get* universe, but the intuitive records—from Ra Ta, to Moses, to Edgar Cayce—deserve to be considered with an open mind and an open heart. In her book, *Our Origin and Destiny*, anthropologist Kathy L. Callahan, Ph.D., maintains that, as our spiritual powers are gradually returning to us, a new intuitive human subspecies may be emerging:

Since the fully integrated human is capable of "knowing" at the spiritual level of the soul, I propose that one name t consider for this new subspecies might be *Homo sapiens intueri*, from the Latin *intueri*, which refers to the "faculty of knowing without the use of rational processes, or immediate cognition," such as that which occurs when the soul

is brought to conscious awareness.

ATLANTIS

Proof of the existence of Atlantis would make many theorists, explorers, philosophers, and spiritual seekers very happy. Still, other than the psychic records of Atlantis, we have little more than circumstantial evidence to guide us—that and the stirrings of the soul's memory that urges us ever toward new discoveries of our ancient past. Atlantis contains perhaps the singlemost important strand of the golden thread, so a brief overview of the disputed lost continent is in order.

Edgar Evans Cayce, the youngest of the great psychic's sons, cites several scientific discoveries in his book *Edgar Cayce on Atlantis* that offer evidence that a mid-Atlantic continent is probable. For example, an article originally published in M.I.T.'s *Technical Engineering News* in 1948 relates the story of a ship's crew that was laying a submarine cable to the depth of two miles in 1898. They lost the end of the cable, and then, while trying to fetch it back with grappling hooks, dragged up some material from the ocean floor. The material proved to have been lava, which scientists verified not only must have originally solidified in the open air, but that it must have been above the water sometime in the last 15,000 years. Edgar Evans Cayce also cites the discovery in 1957 of a deep-sea core taken from a two-mile depth on the Mid-Atlantic Submarine Ridge that contained "exclusively fresh water plants (diatoms)."

In *Fingerprints of the Gods*, a book about the author's search for a "lost civilization," Graham Hancock offers much convincing evidence that Atlantis, or something like it, once existed. He explores evidence such as the "flash-frozen" mammoths in northern Siberia and Alaska and the "90-foot tall fruit trees locked in permafrost deep inside the Arctic Circle." From there, we can compare similarities of pyramid-building, hieroglyphics, embalming, and many other "coincidences" on both sides of the Atlantic. We can also ponder the common mythologies, especially of the Mayans, Aztecs, and Hopi, and ancient stories the world over that speak of a "great flood."

The multitude of arguments for or against the existence of Atlantis are innumerable and fall outside the scope of this work. However, one of the most familiar accounts of Atlantis is that of

Plato, who wrote of it in his *Timaeus* and *Critias* dialogues, describing in detail a continent with a city ringed with canals that had sunk in a volcanic disaster. It seems that Plato had heard the story from Critias around 550 B.C., who had heard it from the Greek lawmaker, Solon, around 600 B.C., who had heard it *during his visit to the city of Sais, in Lower Egypt.* Bauval and Gilbert, in *The Orion Mystery,* make a bold statement about this: "It had been told to Solon by Egyptian priests who said that mysterious people from a place called Atlantis had invaded much of the Mediterranean basin as well as Egypt some 'nine thousand years' ago, and that *records of them still survived in Egypt.*" [italics added]

It should come as no surprise to the reader that most early Roman and Greek writers asserted that the great sages Pythagoras, Plato, and Homer had actually received their philosophies from ancient Egypt. Collaborators Bauval and Hancock, in their book *The Message of the Sphinx,* maintain that those early writers "held it to be axiomatic that the Pharaohs and their priests were guardians of accurate records concerning certain highly significant events that had taken place long, long ago." They maintain that these records were actually seen and studied at Heliopolis (site of the Temple of the Sun), by Herodotus, Solon, and Pythagoras (fifth to sixth centuries B.C.).

While proof of the existence of these records has not yet been discovered in Egypt (some suggest that they were destroyed in the library at Alexandria), one can only wonder if the priests with whom Solon spoke were referring to Ra Ta's "Hall of Records," even at the late date of 600 B.C.

According to the Cayce readings, Atlantis had been a time and place of unlimited creative potential in a beautiful land that was a part of the Garden of Eden. It was when humans began living in physical bodies—the time of Adam. The Atlanteans had wondrous technology, including lighter-than-air ships and electricity. They communicated telepathically and were able to create their reality by projecting thought forms into matter according to their desires.

As to their forms in the physical sense, these were much rather of the nature of *thought forms,* or able to push out *of themselves* in that direction in which its development took shape in thought—much in the way and manner as the amoeba would in the waters of a stagnant bay, or lake, in the present. As

these took form, by the gratifying of their own desire for that as builded or added to the material conditions, they became hardened or set—much in the form of the existent human body of the day . . . (364-3)

The Cayce readings say that many people alive in this century on earth, especially in the United States, are the reincarnated souls of former Atlanteans, and free will was at play then as it is now—the free will to choose oneness or separation. This is because in Atlantis, as long as our desires were divinely aligned, we could still speak with God, face to face. Once we began to desire individual gratification and power, we created "the many" and abandoned "the One."

Ultimately, however, Atlantis self-destructed because it had become a "civilization being disturbed by corruption from within to such measures that the elements join in bringing devastation to a stiff-necked and adulterous people." (5750-1) Many people observe corruption around us today, and, if we were the Atlanteans, we know at subconscious levels that "we have seen this all before." Atlantean corruption, however, actually buried the spirituality of an entire people, forcing humanity to rediscover and rebuild it from scratch. This was corruption at the very core of our ability to make contact with the Universal Consciousness—of our very oneness with God.

According to the readings, Atlantis wasn't destroyed all at once, but underwent three periods during which the "elements" joined together to create upheavals. These periods of destruction reflect, in the earth itself, the spiritual upheavals that were taking place in the hearts and minds of the people. The first of the destructions, around 52,000 B.C., was around the time when "the sons [and daughters] of God saw the daughters [and sons] of men, and saw them that they were fair." (Genesis 6:2 KJV) For at this time of the "Eden of the world" (364-4), the male and female were as one. Atlantis's initial destruction was caused by a misuse of physical forces, gases, and electricity that broke the continent into five smaller islands. The second destruction, around 28,000 B.C., was actually the Great Flood described in Genesis, from which Noah escaped with his retinue in the ark; it was caused by misuse of the divine forces for selfish gain.

The third and final destruction of Atlantis occurred in 10,500 B.C., around the period that Ra Ta began reforming Egypt. This was a time when the remaining Atlanteans fled, migrating westward to Yucatan (ancestors of the Maya, Olmecs, Toltecs, Mexica, Aztecs), North America (the Hopi and Iroquois), Britain (the Druids), the Pyrenees (Basques), and also, of course, eastward to Egypt. It was the Atlantean refugees in Egypt whose bodies and minds had to be corrected in the Temple of Sacrifice and the Temple Beautiful.

Suffice it to say that Graham Hancock and many other supporters of the existence of Atlantis argue strenuously that geologically an entire continent *could* have disappeared over time, many thousands of years ago. Instead of reviewing these arguments, however, we will rediscover and remember our oneness much more directly by exploring the psychic records regarding Atlantis which, in the Cayce readings, number over 600.

What role did our separation from oneness play in the breakup and sinking of Atlantis? The answer to this is "everything," and we will look to the "Children of the Law of One" for the deeper understanding.

THE CHILDREN OF THE LAW OF ONE

Atlantis was initially an island continent located between the present-day Gulf of Mexico and the Mediterranean, and its history spanned over 200,000 years. During that time, the readings say, we consciously separated ourselves from God through aggrandizement of the ego and its selfish desires—we devolved from our Universal Consciousness, toward which we would eventually have to evolve once again—we are now in that unifying process.

The "Nephilim" mentioned in Genesis 6:4 ("giants in the earth" KJV) were actually the Atlanteans:

The Nephilim were on the earth in those days, and also afterward, when the sons of God came in to the daughters of men, and they bore children to them. These were the mighty men that were of old, the men of renown. (Genesis 6:4)

The early Atlanteans still had access to direct communication with God and with the divinity within each other. Over time, however, when rebellious forces began entering human form for selfish purposes, there was division in the earth, and the Atlanteans separated into two groups. One group was the Children of the Law of One, who wanted to remain one with God. The second group was the Sons of Belial, who sought sensual and sensory gratification and materialism. The Children of the Law of One maintained a standard of morality:

Their *standard* was that the soul was given by the Creator or entered from outside sources *into* the projection of the *mental* and spiritual self at the given periods. *That* was the standard of the Law of One, but was *rejected* by the Sons of Belial. (877-26)

What exactly was the Law of One? The readings explain it in a number of ways, but the sense of it is the same. In one reading, it is described as that which applies "even in the experiences of every soul in the present. For, ever has been, ever will be, the law of One the same. 'Love ye in your daily experience. Apply ye in your daily activities the love that ye would have the Father show thee, in thy relationships to thy fellows, do ye know the law of One.'" (497-1) In another reading, the Law of One is actually identified as the Christ Consciousness: " . . . the way of the Law of One—or that manifested in the present as the Christ Consciousness . . . " (884-1) The antiquity of this concept echoes through the words of Jesus, who asks the Father to glorify Him " . . . with the glory which I had with thee before the world was made." (John 17:5)

Following the Law of One (which was easy, until the Sons of Belial offered us the irresistible "apple" of self-worship), we enjoyed physical beauty, excellent health, limitless creative power, and a society dedicated to the Law of One, monitored by temple priests and priestesses who communed directly with God in pure meditation. Atlantean bodies were not the same as ours, but were lighter in density. Before we yielded to the corruptions, we were able to "play" with our powerful imaginative skills that were, then, natural to us:

There are few terms in the present that would indicate the state of consciousness; save that, through the concentration of the group mind of the children of the Law of One, they entered into a fourth-dimensional consciousness—or were absent from the body.

Thus they were able to have that experience of crystallizing, through the Light, the speech from what might well be termed the saint realm, to impart understanding and knowledge to the group thus gathered. (2464-2)

Being able to "crystallize the speech" of the saints on high is an intriguing thought. Imagine, whenever you have a problem, being able to telepathically contact divine beings in the higher realms and have an instant answer! The readings say that communication with God Most High was initially very direct. We were never separate from the radiance of God until we began to create separation through the imagination of our hearts and our free will to do what pleased us.

It may be a cliché to think that the "bad guys" in the world make our lives miserable. But even so, perhaps the Sons of Belial, the original "bad guys," rightfully earned an archetypal place of honor in the mass subconscious, because it was they who broke away from the One for selfish gain and began to worship themselves. They were the first to *actually campaign* for separation and the first to intentionally profit from it. The Children of the Law of One, through the error of their priests and priestesses, followed. As a result, humankind lost its memory of oneness with God. We began to identify more and more with our bodies, our gender, our material possessions, with power, lust, greed, and every other way by which we look for love in all the separate places—instead of seeking it in our oneness with the divine.

With this fundamental difference between the two groups and disagreements about the use of the lower classes (some of whom had been created as slaves and regarded as "things"), the beautiful paradise of Atlantis began to crumble. The airy beauty of its lightly dense buildings and the perfectly formed human bodies of the Atlanteans began to solidify. The telepathic communication channels with the higher planes began to shrivel. More and more, we had to rely on our own ingenuity and folly in order to manage our lives.

As we seek to rejoin the oneness of the universe, it is important to remember that we ourselves were the Atlanteans. We have existed since the beginning, and we have, indeed, been the captains of our fate all along—once we decided to separate from God and forget our origin in oneness. Curiously, we have to look to the time before Adam—before we lived in physical bodies—in order to remember our origin.

LEMURIAN MEMORIES

From Atlantis, we follow the golden thread even further back, to the beginnings of our conscious separation from God. The readings say that the earth is 10,500,000 years old and that there were, in fact, many civilizations and "lost lands" upon which souls imaginatively cocreated in the material world. At the time when humankind began to live in human bodies, the surface of the planet was vastly different from the world we know today:

The Nile entered into the Atlantic Ocean. What is now the Sahara was an inhabited land and very fertile. What is now the central portion of this country, or the Mississippi basin, was then all in the ocean . . . That along the Atlantic board formed the outer portion then, or the lowlands of Atlantis. The Andean, or the Pacific coast of South America, occupied then the extreme western portion of Lemuria. (364-13)

The paleontological records offer enough evidence to show that such earth changes were possible, even likely. However, Lemuria, the lost Pacific continent named in the reading above, predates Atlantis. While Lemuria can be identified in mythological literature, author James Churchward discovered fascinating records which support the probability that there was a mid-Pacific continent. Although he was criticized for the "quasi-science" he used to substantiate it (by de Camp and others), these records are an important contribution to our understanding of our early history in the earth.

Chiefly, Churchward's records consisted of the Naacal tablets in India, written with Naga symbols, that he had studied in the late 1800s. In his well-known book, *The Lost Continent of Mu*, he claimed he was instructed by an Indian sage that the tablets had been written in Lemuria and carried to India by way of Burma. Secondly, Churchward studied a set of 2,400 "tablets" found in Mexico in the 1910s by an engineer named William Niven. In addition to Churchward's books, published in the early part of this century, the work of Augustus Le Plongeon provides a significant precedent for the probability of a Pacific continent. He was a physician who dedicated his life to the exploration of Mayan culture and language. His study of the *Troano Codex* (one of only three Mayan books that survived the bibliopyres of the Spanish conquerers), convinced him that it contained the history of an ancient civilization to the West.

The Cayce readings tell us that the Lemurians were the predecessors of the Children of the Law of One. In Lemuria, we were closer to God—we knew God and communicated with God, basking in the light of pure knowledge without distortion. We were closer in awareness and closer in the certainty, the consciousness, that we were a part of God. In fact, our bodies were

not yet dense and could hardly be called physical. We would
come and go in the wondrous plane of manifestation: everything
we dreamed or imagined became a reality, if we so willed it, for
"free will" was a part of our oneness with divinity—then, as now.
We had complete freedom to enter and leave our early bodies
and began making the mistakes we would continue later, in
Atlantis, and in our own time:

**This was before the sojourn of peoples in perfect body form;
rather when they may be said to have been able to—through
those developments of the period—be in the body or out of the
body and act upon materiality. In the spirit or in flesh these
made those things, those influences, that brought destruction;
for the atmospheric pressure in the earth in the period was
quite different from that experienced by the physical being of
today. (436-2)**

During the immeasurable thousands of centuries of Lemuria's
existence, we were the children of God, still free to come and go
in heavenly realms. But the experience of paradise, we are to
understand, was meant to be eternal, ever since we began to play
and experiment with our own creativity:

**When the Creative Forces, God, made then the first man—or
God-man—he was the beginning of the Sons of God. Then those
souls who entered through a channel made by God—not by
thought, not by desire, not by lust, not by things that separated
continually—were the Sons of God, the Daughters of God. (262-
119)**

We can accept that, at the soul level, our oneness with God
has never actually ended, but we have created for ourselves a
world of material desires and spiritual problems, and accepted
them as our reality. We have accepted our apparent separation
as the truth of our existence, without believing as fully in the al-
ternative. Where separation is concerned, the readings tell us
something extraordinary that happened to the sexes during this
time. After the separations of gender occurred, it wouldn't become "a man's world" for a very long time:

**In that experience the entity was in the same sex as at
present, but among those that were the leaders; for *then* the
women *ruled*—rather than men. (630-2)**

This entire process began as the paradise we knew in the
heavens began to take on form and substance in the earth
through our creative experimentation. In Lemuria, the body and

its pleasures, the joy of self-identity were too fascinating to resist. As long as we remained one with our Creator, "we were not ashamed":

The entity was among those that journeyed to the land of the Incal as now called . . . For the entity then was a princess that lost its way from the daughters of the Law of One of those that made for the aggrandizing of the bodily forces and influences for position and power, the temples of fame, the temples of beauty, the hoarding of wealth, the hoarding of those mediums of exchange that were not only beautiful in their own selves but as to the light, as to the influence same had upon the minds of others. (1183-1)

It is true, according to the readings, that Atlantis sank—in three different periods of destruction. But Lemuria, the Pacific continent, disappeared first. For a time, they coexisted, but when Lemuria began to self-destruct, what was about to occur became apparent to the knowledgeable, intuitive Children of God:

Before that we find the entity was in that land now known as Mu, or the vanished land of the Pacific, the Peaceful; during those periods when many of those had risen to power when there were being those banishments and preparations for the preserving; for they had known that the land must be soon broken up. (630-2)

Preserving? As their land was sinking, they knew they had to migrate to Atlantis. Furthermore, they knew that they had to take with them the principles of the One—the very records that would be conveyed from Atlantis to Egypt, perhaps a hundred thousand years in the future.

The life readings give us several clues as to how, in Lemuria, we began to lose sight of God and lose our memory of oneness (the quotations below are from reading 851-2):

. . . activities in the land . . . had brought destructive forces through the separations from those things that made for the love of the individual for the gratifying of selfish motives.

Before that we find the entity was in that land now known as the American, during those periods when there were the changes that had brought about the sinking of Mu or Lemuria, or those peoples in the periods who had changed to what is now a portion of the Rocky Mountain area; Arizona, New Mexico, portions of Nevada and Utah.

The entity then was among the princesses of the land that

established there the teachings of the Law of *One*, from the activities in the land which had brought destructive forces through the separations from those things that made for the love of the individual for the gratifying of selfish motives.

The readings tell us that "All souls were created in the beginning, and are finding their way back" to God. (3744-5) In other words, as souls, we have all been part of the entire creation process. We have all been a part of the devolution from oneness, the separation from God, and the cycles of learning we entered when we first took on physical bodies.

We'll look at the actual moment of creation itself in the next chapter. However, the following reading will give us a head start, for it explains how Christ entered the earth during the Piscean Age, to become the pattern, once again, for regaining oneness with the Father. The reading also summarizes how we abused our awareness, our spiritual knowledge, in those past civilizations.

(Q) What will the Aquarian Age mean to mankind as regards physical, mental and spiritual development? Is the Aquarian Age described as the "Age of the Lily" and why?

(A) . . . In the Piscean Age, in the center of same, we had the entrance of Emmanuel or God among men, see? What did that mean? The same will be meant by the full consciousness of the ability to communicate with . . . the relationships to the Creative Forces and the uses of same in material environs. This awareness during the era or age in the age of Atlantis and Lemuria or Mu brought what? Destruction to man, and his beginning of the needs of the journey up through that of selfishness. (1602-3)

We lost our memory of oneness with God—this is how we traded the Garden of Eden for the knowledge of good and evil. It is the story of the "Fall of Mankind" and our status in regaining all that we have lost. Cayce's hopeful vision is that in that "regaining," we will have also matured as souls, and we can become the conscious, cocreative beings that God originally intended, yet which we have never before achieved.

We have traced the golden thread of oneness from the present back to the teachings of Jesus and the patriarchs who paved the way for His coming. We have also seen how the trail of oneness draws us back through Egyptian history. We have traveled beyond recorded history, too, through the psychic records to the time before the sinking of continents. We will now seek the memory of our oneness during the time before we lived in the atmospheres of earth, on back to the beginning of our spiritual history.

But, first, we need a "reality check."

WRITTEN OVER THE DOOR
OF THE TEMPLE BEAUTIFUL

As you seek to enter the temple of your own oneness with God, enter into prayer and meditation with these affirmations from reading 281-25. Accept the attitude of gratitude and faith conveyed through them, for these we once spoke upon entering the Temple Beautiful.

"Laying aside those things that easily beset the sons [and daughters] of men, ye as ye enter here, put thy whole trust in the one God, that ye may be all things unto all men [and women], thereby crucifying thine own desires that they—thy brethren—may know the Lord their God." (281-25)

The FIRST: LORD, THOU ART MY DWELLING PLACE. ABIDE THOU, O GOD, IN THE TEMPLE OF MY BODY, THAT IT MAY BE WHOLLY AS THOU WOULD HAVE IT.

The SECOND: LET THE JOY OF THE LORD FILL MY MIND, MY BODY, QUICKENING THE SPIRIT, THAT THE DEEDS THAT ARE DONE MAY BE ACCEPTABLE IN HIS SIGHT.

The THIRD: LORD, KEEP THOU MY WAYS. LET ME FIND JOY AND PLEASURE IN MANIFESTING SUCH A LIFE THAT IT MAY GIVE HOPE AND HELP AND CHEER TO OTHERS.

The FOURTH: LORD, THE MAKER OF HEAVEN AND EARTH, THE GIVER OF THE CHRIST IN THE HEARTS OF MEN, QUICKEN THOU THE SPIRIT WITHIN, THAT THY LIGHT, THY LOVE, MAY BE MANIFESTED THROUGH ME.

The FIFTH: LORD, THOU ART MY REDEEMER. IN THE CHRIST DO WE SEEK TO KNOW THEE THE BETTER. LET LOVE AND HEALTH, LET JOY AND PROSPERITY OF THE LORD QUICKEN MY WAYS.

The SIXTH: LORD, THOU ART THE GIVER OF ALL GOOD AND PERFECT GIFTS. MAY THE LIGHT OF THY COUNTENANCE IN CHRIST SHINE UPON ME NOW, MAKING FOR THE MANIFES-

TATIONS OF THE LOVE THOU HAST PROMISED IN HIM.

The SEVENTH: LORD, MAKER OF HEAVEN AND EARTH AND ALL THEREIN. LET THE LOVE OF THE CHRIST BE MY GUIDE, THAT MY BODY, MY MIND, MAY BE WHOLE IN THEE: AND THUS BE THE CHANNEL OF A BLESSING TO OTHERS.

The EIGHTH: LORD, THOU ART MY DWELLING PLACE. QUICKEN THE SPIRIT WITHIN ME THAT THOU MAY HAVE THY WAY WITH ME, THAT I MAY BE THE GREATER CHANNEL OF BLESSINGS TO OTHERS.

The NINTH that as written over the door of the Temple Beautiful:
PARCOI SO SUNO CUM [?].
LORD, LEAD THOU THE WAY.
I COMMIT MY BODY, MY MIND, TO BE ONE WITH THEE.

Chapter 5

BEFORE THE WORLD WAS

ONE WITH ALPHA AND OMEGA

As daunting as it may seem to comprehend the oneness of God, it is easier than we might think to *experience* it through our feelings. To speed us along our way, it will help to gain a sense of the difference between "manifest" and "unmanifest" reality. While the topic may appear to be a foray into Eastern philosophy, we need look no further than the Bible for a starting point.

In the beginning, God divided the darkness from the light. The idea of manifestation was implicit here, simply because anything that possesses identity apart from the whole is "manifest." Another clue to manifest and unmanifest reality that can be seen is when God warned the people not to make graven images of " . . . anything that is in heaven above, or that is in the earth beneath, or that is in the water under the earth . . . " (Exodus 20:4) Essentially, all that is real is being either manifest or unmanifest. This is the simplest possible concept in the universe, save that of oneness itself. Simple logic tells us that "all that is—*is*," whether or not we can perceive it. There is nothing else but the universe—whatever it may be in its totality.

"Manifest reality" is all that is perceived, imagined, thought, or described, such as the visible world, our thoughts and feelings, or each other. "Unmanifest reality" is that which is unseen or hidden—all that God's mind perceives and that ours do not. Another example from the Bible that acknowledges both kinds of reality is Paul's definition of faith: " . . . the assurance of things hoped for, the conviction of things not seen. For by it the men of old received divine approval." (Hebrews 11:1)

How do we distinguish between the "seen" and the "unseen"? Psychologists are quick to point out that our very sense perceptions are untrustworthy. Still, we will never cease to try interpreting all that manifests itself to us. As for the unmanifest, we do not know its scope—and it doesn't matter whether we do or not. We are content with evidence, even though we don't necessarily know how to interpret it—even the "evidence of things not seen." (Hebrews 11:1 KJV) The important fact to remember, however, is that there is nothing beyond manifest and unmanifest reality— it is all reality. Reality, whatever it is, *in toto*, is One.

Let's look more closely at this idea, because it plays an important part in a practical understanding of oneness. The Cayce readings use the word "manifestation" in order to explain just what occurred "in the beginning."

Hence, every form of life that man sees in a material world is an essence or manifestation of the Creator; not the Creator, but a manifestation of a first cause—and in its own sphere, its own consciousness of its activity in that plane or sphere ... What *is* Life? A manifestation of the first cause—God! (5753-1)

The distinction between the manifest and unmanifest should be understood in terms of our knowledge and our thoughts, because the manifest reality of the mind consists of our ideas, feelings, senses, and the very processes of thinking. The unmanifest reality of the mind includes all that resides in the subconscious, unconscious, and most certainly the superconscious—that plane of oneness with God's mind, the Universal Consciousness.

"Know, rather," say the Cayce readings, "that the unseen influences in the experience of every soul are greater than those that are seen." (1531-1) This observation is important to remember whenever we contemplate the power and love of God—or even our own divinity—manifest or unmanifest, because the concepts are two of the primary archetypes of consciousness itself. And yet, once again from the Bible, all is one, because all reality will eventually become manifest:

... nothing is covered that will not be revealed, or hidden that will not be known. (Matthew 10:26)

The evidence is overwhelming that we share an inherent oneness with God—you, I, and everyone else, whether or not we consciously perceive it. The inherent oneness itself, like everything else that we don't know, is an unmanifest part of ourselves—an unmanifest reality within us that we can only know with increased awareness of the "unseen." Human beings do, indeed, demonstrate evidence of oneness. It's just that when we do, we are usually not aware of it. Even the saints among us find it difficult to express their experience of oneness in words. Hence, the necessity for "holy languages," such as Sanskrit, music, and poetry. Our saints among us do not try to express oneness in words. They express it by performing acts that demonstrate its presence in their hearts and minds, for they know how to:

Let your light so shine before men, that they may see your good works and give glory to your Father who is in heaven. (Matthew 5:16)

The divine within each of us is the same universal helping hand from out of the unfathomable totality of oneness, which we can feel during those moments when we receive unexpected help, when we realize that the love of God is "nudging us, tugging at our hands, or turning our heads," or, as the readings put it, when we receive "urges from the unseen."

In what faith means to the individual, as we have faith in the substance, or that which is hoped for, with the evidences from things seen or of things unseen. As in this, the desire of the heart or issues of life to be the assistance not from self, but even as the Maker gives, as is given that love is law. Law is love. Love is giving. Giving is as God, the Maker. (3744-2)

If God is love, then we can manifest our "oneness-with-love." This is not the same as intellectual understanding, but performing acts that demonstrate love's presence in our hearts. So it is with the unmanifest aspects of God, who manifests love to us by demonstrating it. Knowing love within us is knowing love within God. God manifests love through the prophets, when we refuse to hear God any other way. We are all one in the intuitive, vibrant, formless energy of love. All love, if it is love, is the same. *Love is One.*

Oneness is easy to accept, and even to rely on, if we can agree that we, the created, cannot think beyond the bounds of God's thought, because God is boundless. God is the First Cause, the Universal Consciousness inside which all that is exists. God is the Universal Consciousness, therefore, within which resides all consciousness, even ours. The key to experiencing oneness is realizing that we don't have to understand everything that oneness encompasses. Oneness certainly includes manifest reality *and* unmanifest reality—all matter, all thought, all imagination, and all that is unseen. Oneness encompasses that which is temporary, such as our bodies and the forms that we create in the world. Oneness includes all that is permanent, such as our immortal souls, unified in oneness together with God, which we have had since the beginning.

If we could actually remember "the beginning," when we were created, remembering our oneness should be instantaneous. In principle, such an experience should be easy to define: before we were created—bursting forth in joy from the First Cause in order to be companions—oneness was quite simply "knowing" that we were all one. There was no consciousness other than our Universal Consciousness of pure love for the Creator.

In our original state, time did not exist. We can relate to a state without time by recalling intense instances in our lives, for example, when we find ourselves reacting in an emergency, while dreaming, or during the peak of orgasm. It was the timeless epoch when we were first released into self-awareness, all one with the beginning as well as the end, our destiny—one with Alpha and Omega in eternal life.

This was truly the glory that was in the beginning when at first we were created and when light (consciousness itself) was divided from the darkness by the First Cause. This was the glory we had before "before the world was made," (John 17:5) and before we became distracted by our own beauty, creativity, and the initial *fun* of selfishness. It was before stress and worry. Before fear and before hate had ever been thought of.

THE FIRSTBORN AND THE WAY BACK

When did we first exist? It must have been before we first alighted in the atmospheres of substance as Lemurian thought forms or projected ourselves into denser bodies of flesh in Atlantis. Edgar Cayce was once asked, "When did I first exist as a separate entity?" He answered that "The first existence . . . was in the MIND of the Creator, as all souls became a part of the creation. As to time, this would be in the beginning. When was the beginning? *First consciousness.*" (2925-1) [italics added]

At the moment of our creation, we were instantaneously infused with consciousness amid an ecstatic bloom of billions of souls, duplicate divine sparks, conscious entities that reacted to self-consciousness in different ways. If we had not reacted differently, noticed our individuality, we would have remained unmanifest—indistinguishable from the One. At that moment, each of us, without gender, without dimension, substance, or form, possessed only I AM awareness and the radiant bliss which was knowing oneness with God, in perfection, face to face:

. . . the gift of God to man is an *individual* soul that may be one *with* Him, and that may know itself to be one with Him and yet individual in itself, with the attributes *of* the whole, yet *not* the whole. (262-11)

We have been aware of self and God ever since the beginning. *In the beginning*—this phrase is the root of our oneness and the key to our remembering it. There was nothing to clutter or cloud our thoughts, as our very egos were consumed in the flame of our love for the Creator. According to Lytle Robinson, in his *Edgar Cayce's Story of the Origin and Destiny of Man*, the First Cause was the oneness of all force, all manifestation. The *second cause* was the initiative of the Creative Forces to create and a desire for companionship. Spirit moved, and out spun separate vibrations, little models of God's consciousness—we, who are God's children.

"But not for long did the will of the souls remain the will of their Source," writes Robinson. "They began to experiment, fascinated with the power of their own creative individuality. Desire and self-aggrandizement gave birth to the destructive—that which was opposed to goodness, the opposite of God's will. By magnifying their own will and independence, the selfishness of the ego came into being. It was this turning away from God's will that brought about the downfall, the separation, the end of the state of perfection. This was the Revolt of the Angels, or the Fall of Man."

This original oneness—total consumption by and absorption of God—has never left us. Through our own creative deeds, however, we have drifted away from oneness, because we had the power either to remain in the pure Christ pattern or to yield to that "influence that *separates* the inner self from being aware of the oneness of all force and power that manifests itself in the earth . . . " (903-23)

While observing the activities of animal forms, we separated into sexes. Rebellious desires led us further into separation from

God and this led to our forgetting. Through the karma we created—the causes and effects of our actions—we also forgot our
oneness with each other. Hence destructions of the civilizations
of Lemuria, Atlantis, and others. We encrusted the truth of our
oneness with our own artificial creations in the earth in which
we began to trust and to believe. We experimented until we created a world of materiality and Lilliputian power struggles.

As we, the children of God, entrapped ourselves in matter, our
Creator had to do something in order to bring us back into Universal Consciousness and make our will one again, with the
Creator's will. God would have to take action in order to bring us
back to eternal life. God would do this through the initiative of
what the readings call the "Firstborn," which led to the Judeo-
Christian revolution of the "one God," and by making the Word
flesh in the person of the Messiah. This was a plan that began
even before Adam.

As souls, we have all existed since the beginning, when we
were created as companions to God. We were created along with
the "Firstborn," which is the master pattern of Christ (finally
demonstrated on earth in the person of Jesus) and which all
people, whatever their path, work toward reconstructing or remembering within themselves.

**Thus is He the only begotten, the firstborn, the first to know
flesh, the first to purify it. (1158-5)**

The readings identify the Firstborn as Amilius (a name Jesus'
soul bore when He was a ruler in Atlantis), and Amilius is the
Master Soul—a spark that was created perfect, as we were all created perfect, in the beginning. The readings trace the fascinating
spiritual journey of Amilius all the way to His life as Jesus of
Nazareth—He who has followed us since the beginning, so that
He could show us the way back.

**Then, as the sons of God came together and saw in the earth
the unspeakable conditions becoming more and more for self-
indulgence, self-glorifications, the ability to procreate through
the very forces of their activity, we find that our Lord, our
Brother, *chose* to measure up, to earn, to *attain* that companionship for man with the Father through the overcoming of *self*
in the physical plane. (262-115)**

This takes us back to the time of the "first creation" as discussed in chapter 2, before we wore bodies of flesh. As we began
to turn away from the light, becoming entangled with our own

miscreations, there was no consistency in the thought forms we were projecting or in our mental activities. Such was chaos—the chaos *we ourselves* began to create—as we became gradually imprisoned in matter, creating bizarre forms and then following after them into denser experiences. Amilius knew what He had to do. The only way was for Him to follow after us, become immersed in matter Himself, and then, freeing Himself, lead us back to the one true God.

Before the plan could begin, certain consistencies had to be incorporated in the earth. The earth had to be separated from the firmament; the dry land separated from the waters. The bodies into which the souls were projecting themselves had to be consolidated into a stable form with two genders, hence Adam, the first "flesh man."

We didn't, in fact, begin as awkward primates, but as lithe souls—spiritual beings who entrapped themselves in flesh. Our present physical form was, indeed, created by God, with the needed physical tools—fingers, arms, legs, eyes, and ears—for survival in the material world. Within that body, God placed seven spiritual centers by which we would always be able to access a connection with our Creator, no matter how far we strayed. These centers are called *chakras* in Sanskrit; *chakra* means "wheel." They are the centers of spiritual energy in our bodies by which we maintain communication lines with the divine—no matter how deeply submerged their presence may be from our awareness. (The Cayce perspective on the spiritual centers is explained in *Meditation and the Mind of Man*, by Herbert B. Puryear, Ph.D., and Mark Thurston, Ph.D. See Selected Reading List at the back of this book.)

This was a perfect body by which humankind could eventually free itself from its selfish follies and return to the happy, *manifest* reality of oneness that we knew in the beginning.

This was the plan by which Amilius devised for us a means of escape from the material plane—the path of the Christ—and the plan began with His first incarnation as Adam.

This was not the first spiritual influence, spiritual body, spiritual manifestation in the earth, but the first man—flesh and blood; the first carnal house, the first amenable body to the laws of the plane in its position in the universe ... And man's development began through the laws of the generations in the earth; thus the development, retardment, or the alterations in those

positions in a material plane. (5749-3)

The Firstborn actually descended initially into all that the earth plane had to offer, even the loss of Eden and eating of the Tree of the Knowledge of Good and Evil. But that's not all. This Master Soul then continued to incarnate, participating in every step of human activity throughout history. Amilius postponed His heaven, in order to lead the flock back to God. He could only do this by first losing His way—succumbing to all the appetites and follies by which humanity had beguiled itself. He accomplished this with the aid of spiritually minded soul-entities from the higher realms, "the sons of the Most High," referred to in the readings as the "Brotherhood" or "White Brotherhood."

These divine entities were souls who had either freed themselves early from the magnetism of the material world or who had managed to avoid creating karma and the need for reincarnation. Members of the Brotherhood guided the construction of the Great Pyramid as a Hall of Initiation, in which Jesus would receive training during the years of His "absence" after the age of twelve. In fact, the Cayce eadings state that records of the Christ about the time He spent there are contained in an as-yet-undiscovered pyramid under the sand on the Gizeh plateau (5749-2). The Brotherhood also guided the Essene sect, which prepared for the incarnation of Jesus and, according to the readings, chose and trained Mary to be His mother.

The plan of Amilius becomes crystal clear when we recall Jesus saying, "No one has ascended into heaven but he who descended from heaven, the Son of man." (John 3:13) The Cayce readings offer insight in the way of an explanation:

Though man be far afield, then, though he may have erred, there is established that which makes for a closer, closer walk with Him, through that one who experienced all those turmoils, strifes, desires, urges that may be the lot of man in the earth. (5749-6)

While embodied in the earth just like we, the lost lambs, he perfected himself and freed himself through successive incarnations. The readings tell us that Amilius lived as Adam, but also as other notables during critical events that led the way for the coming of the Messiah:

(Q) Please list the names of the incarnations of the Christ, and of Jesus, indicating where the development of the man Jesus began.

(A) First, in the beginning, of course; and then as Enoch, Melchizedek, in the perfection. Then in the earth of Joseph, Joshua, Jeshua, Jesus. (5749-14)

The implications of the Lord's presence throughout human history are as astounding as they are comforting. He was sent to find His sheep, right from the very beginning.

ENOCH, HERMES, AND MELCHIZEDEK

As Enoch, the Firstborn learned to escape death (Genesis 5:24), for Enoch "was not, for God took him" ("taken up," KJV) without dying. Author and researcher Glenn Sanderfur, in his book *Lives of the Master*, presents a fascinating and detailed examination of the embodiments the "Jesus soul" took on in order to complete His service to the human race. Among the support he presents is that, while Jesus is called the "Son of Man" in the New Testament, Enoch is called the "Son of Man" in the revelatory apochryphal *First Book of Enoch*. Once considered a part of the church canon, this book is the first to identify a preexisting Messiah and a Second Coming. Sanderfur provides a revealing excerpt from another apochryphal book, the *Second Book of Adam and Eve* (*SBAE*), concerning the end of Enoch's life:

Thus, because Enoch was in the light of God, he found himself out of the reach of death; until God would have him die. (*SBAE* XXII:8-9)

This quotation opens the door to the prospect that Enoch's "death" would be reserved for the death as Jesus on the cross.

In addition to Enoch, the readings indicate that the Firstborn also lived as the architect, Hermes, who worked with Araaraart and Ra Ta to build the Great Pyramid and the Great Sphinx for preserving the records of Atlantis. Later identified as "Trismegistus," or "thrice great" by the Greeks, both Hermes and Jesus have been called "The Great Initiator." This, alone, should not satisfy even those who accept the possibility of Jesus having had several incarnations. However, writings attributed to Hermes are astonishingly familiar.

The Hermetic writings actually predate Moses—exactly when, no one knows. Many claim that these writings only originated in the second century A.D., while others, such as translator John D. Chambers, identify Hermes as "an Egyptian sage or succession of sages, who, since the time of Plato, has been identified with the Thoth [the god of learning, wisdom, and magic] . . . of that people." The writings of Hermes contain many links to Christ and His teachings, and are collectively called *The Poemandres*, which significantly translates from the Greek as the "Shepherd of Men."

In *Lives of the Master,* Sanderfur cites Lactantius (fourth century A.D.), who "taught that the Hermetic writings were based upon the work of an Egyptian seer whose references to a 'son of God' were prophetic of Christ. He compared wording in the Hermetica with certain passages in the Gospel of John . . . " John D. Chambers's translation of *The Poemandres* provides powerful evidence of the direct relationship between Hermes and Christ:

Knowest thou not that thou has been born God and Son of the One, which also I? (*Poemandres* VIII:14)

The Mind . . . is of the very essence of God; if indeed there is any essence of God, and of what quality this may be, He alone hath accurately known. The Mind then is not cut off from the Essentiality of The Godhead but united, just as the light of the Sun. But this the Mind in men indeed is God. (*Poemandres* VII:1)

In another passage, Hermes names the "generator of the Regeneration" as "The Son of God; One Man by the Will of God." (*Poemandres* XIII:4) Sanderfur quotes a Naassene document cited by Hippolytus of Rome (around A.D. 200), in which Hermes is called "the Logos and identified with both Adam and Christ."

The path from Adam to Enoch, Enoch to Amilius, and Amilius to Hermes spirals us forward along the golden thread once again to the time of Ra Ta, in which the secrets of the Universal Consciousness—the history of human consciousness and the records thereof—are hidden in the Gizeh plateau in buildings designed by Hermes—all part of the preparation for the coming of the Messiah, as well as the Second Coming. But there is one more earthly sojourn of the Firstborn that will help us connect directly back to our oneness in the beginning and from the beginning back to the present: that sojourn was as the priest, Melchizedek.

A Psalm of David (110:4) praises what the Lord said to David's Lord: "The LORD has sworn and will not change his mind, 'You are a priest for ever after the order of Melchiz'edek.'" In Genesis 14:18-20, we learn little more about Melchizedek than that Abraham himself paid tithes to him. In the seventh chapter of his Epistle to the Hebrews, however, Paul fills us in on the facts about this mysterious figure.

For this Melchiz'edek, king of Salem, priest of the Most High God, met Abraham returning from the slaughter of the kings and blessed him; and to him Abraham apportioned a tenth part of everything. He is first, by translation of his name, king of righteousness, and then he is also king of Salem, that is, king of peace. He is without father or mother or genealogy, and has neither beginning of days nor end of life, but resembling the Son of God he continues a priest for ever. (Hebrews 7:1-3)

Melchizedek, therefore, was a king in his own right and blessed Abraham. He is a type of priest, like Jesus, who lives forever. Levi, as yet unborn, would pay tithes to Melchizedek in Abraham's name. Like Jesus, he was a priest ordained by God, not by man. Finally, that his priesthood cannot be interrupted by death because "he continues a priest for ever." (It is interesting to note that reading 262-55 states that it was actually Melchizedek who wrote the Book of Job.)

Melchizedek was without father and without mother, without days or years. The point about Melchizedek that is most relevant to our finding of oneness again is the important fact that Jesus said that He had *manifested Himself to Abraham* and *knew* him:

"Your father Abraham rejoiced that he was to see my day; he saw it and was glad." The Jews then said to him, "You are not yet fifty years old, and have you seen Abraham?" Jesus said to them, "Truly, truly, I say to you, before Abraham was, I am." (John 8:56-58)

According to the readings, the Firstborn also lived as Asaph, a scribe who penned some of the Psalms, and Joseph, son of Jacob and Rachael, who was abducted by his brothers *and sold into slavery in Egypt*. He was Joshua, who was the channel through which Moses received the Ten Commandments (5023-2). He was also Zend, who founded Zoroastrianism, and the priest Jeshua, who helped lead the Babylonian captives back to Judah.

The Firstborn, then, played a vital role in every aspect of human resurrection from the Fall of Humankind to the reestablishing of the Law of One in Egypt through Ra Ta and preserved it in the Hall of Records. He descended right along with us into the trap of the earth, working with the "sons of the Most High." He actually helped prepare for his *own* coming, by which he would lead us all to our personal Christhood—the Universal Consciousness, as it was in the beginning, "For the Son of man is come to save that which was lost." (Matthew 18:11 KJV) As for the role Jesus plays even now in our rediscovery of oneness, the Edgar Cayce readings offer this cogent advice:

First find thyself. Apply thyself in such a way and manner as to know what ye will do with this man, Jesus of Nazareth— Jeshua of Jerusalem, Joshua in Shiloh, Joseph in the court of Pharaoh, Melchizedek, as he blessed Abraham, Enoch as he warned the people, Adam as he listened to Eve. (3054-4)

The story of Amilius is rich in helpful insights, especially in this age which, the readings maintain, is the eve of the Second Coming. The risen Jesus Christ, at once the Firstborn and the Messiah, will soon reveal the next step in His great plan. All He asked is that we be ready:

Therefore you also must be ready; for the Son of man is coming at an hour you do not expect. (Matthew 24:44)

ONENESS HAPPENS

With the Christhood of the Firstborn radiantly established in the person of Jesus of Nazareth, the libraries and pulpits of the world abound with advice and instruction as to how we can follow Jesus' lead. Whether we realize it or not, we humans are on the road to discovering our own connection to Universal Consciousness and earning our own Christhood.

The world has been studying and interpreting Jesus' words for two thousand years, coming together, splitting apart, making war, and making peace in His name. And yet, through Christ, we shall attain our oneness. As Jesus said, "I am the way, and the truth, and the life; no one comes to the Father, but by me." (John 14:6) By this, He means that we can only go to the Father within, through our personal Christhood within.

(Q) Should the Christ Consciousness be described as the awareness within each soul, imprinted in pattern on the mind and waiting to be awakened by the will, of the soul's oneness with God?

(A) Correct. That's the idea exactly! (5749-14)

The psychic records go a long way in showing us how we can actually remember this oneness with God. They show us how to rejoin the Universal Consciousness in order to reawaken the central divinity of our nature and cross the troubled waters of our own miscreation. In the readings, we find a springboard from which we can plunge into the crystalline depths of Universal Consciousness.

With desire and discipline, we can eventually dive into the purity of *samadhi* that Gautama revealed or swoon with the saints in ecstatic remembrance of our oneness with God. In the depths of Universal Consciousness, we will find the pattern of Christ, which was fixed forever by Jesus and resides sleeping within our very hearts. At the very least, we can learn, with grace, how to unite our lives with the divine plan, more clearly understand the guidance we receive "from the unseen," and begin to heal the hurt we have caused for ourselves by our choices to separate from God. Successes occur all the time, and there is plenty of evidence to convince us.

In his classic study in the evolution of the human mind, *Cosmic Consciousness*, early twentieth-century philosopher Richard Maurice Bucke, M.D., offered a number of examples of people who had made contact with "cosmic consciousness," which is what he called the Universal Consciousness. He referred to "cosmic consciousness" as our "sense of immortality, a consciousness of eternal life, not a conviction that he shall have this, but the consciousness that he has it already."

Bucke maintained that Buddha's Enlightenment under the bodhi tree was actually his realization of "cosmic consciousness," and that Jesus was referring to it whenever he mentioned "the Kingdom of God" or "the Kingdom of Heaven." Bucke described Saul's conversion on the road to Damascus and Muhammad's *Al Kader* (night of The Divine Decree) as realizations of "cosmic consciousness." Likewise was Moses' experience on Mount Sinai with the tablets of stone. After he returned, he did not realize "that the skin of his face shone because he had been talking with God." (Exodus 34:29)

In the world of distractions and illusions, these great prophets, as well as the Messiah Himself, knew oneness with the Universal Consciousness. To them, the truth became known, and they shared it with humankind to show us the way back to Alpha, forward to Omega.

But what does this mean to us, as individuals? How can we, too, have such an awakening? Furthermore, is it necessary that we have a conversion, an illumination, a "cosmic consciousness" experience, like Saul, for example, in order to experience oneness or to contact the Universal Consciousness? The answer that Bucke provides is more satisfying than we might expect, because he didn't stop with the saints and prophets.

He showed dramatic evidence from their writings that Roger Bacon, Spinoza, Thoreau, Emerson, William Blake, Socrates, Pascal, de Balzac, Whitman, and many other literary notables wrote of such an experience:

> As in a swoon, one instant,
> Another sun, ineffable full-dazzles me,
> And all the orbs I knew, and brighter, unknown orbs;
> One instant of the future land, Heaven's land.
> —Walt Whitman

Bucke also showed a number of testimonies from ordinary men and women that such experiences are not unique to saints and philosophers. His book shares many personal testimonies of architects, ministers, musicians, housewives, and physicians—people just like you and me.

He described a doctor, J.B.B., who "entered into Cosmic Consciousness in 1855, at the age of thirty-eight years." The doctor had had a near-death experience (NDE); he had died and left his body for twenty minutes. After the experience, he had access to great truths. Bucke also tells of a laborer, C.P., who achieved cosmic consciousness at age thirty-seven, suddenly finding himself able to interpret remarkable dreams. He became Christlike to those around him and exhibited an uncanny ability to understand the scriptures. A woman, C.Y.E., who had married in 1891, described the effects of her experience with cosmic consciousness, observing that her subjective light was visible and that she had realized a moral elevation, intellectual illumination, a sense of immortality, and an absence of fear about death.

Naturally, people of all times and places have had such experiences, be they called "revelation," "psychic," "transcendental," or "cosmic." In our day, a hundred years after Bucke's research, mainstream people are more aware than ever of NDEs, prophetic dreams, and other paranormal nudges from the Universal Consciousness.

But dramatic experiences, such as those above, are not necessary, nor should they be considered the barometer of one's success in contacting the Universal Consciousness. In the following chapters we will look at specific techniques by which you can

increase the frequency and your receptivity to positive influences from the Universal Consciousness. Before we do, however,
let's take a brief look at how the Cayce readings define the mind
and how it works, relative to the Universal Consciousness.

SOUL TALK

The Edgar Cayce readings often repeat the point that all is one
and that Universal Consciousness is accessible to all. In reading
2828-2, Cayce said, "Life itself is the consciousness, the awareness of that oneness of that Universal Consciousness in the
earth." This is an echo of what Jesus promised to us "for behold,
the kingdom of God is in the midst of you." (Luke 17:21)

The first step in opening ourselves to the influence of Universal Consciousness is to realize that we are not our bodies—that
we are spiritual beings who choose to live within these shells of
flesh and use a marvelous divine tool to make our lives whatever
we wish—*the mind*. But while we use our minds, we are not our
minds—we are souls, pure consciousness entity and identity. As
souls, we are eternal.

This is the "body, mind, spirit" principle from the Cayce readings that has liberated many thousands of people from ignorance about who we are. " . . . spirit is the life; the mind is the
builder; the physical is the result" (349-4), say the readings, and
it is also the key to discovering our oneness. God is one, and yet
we know a trinity of aspects of God. We, too, are one—made in
God's image—and have this triune nature as well. The body
grows old, dies, and decomposes. The soul continues on forever
and cannot be destroyed. Life after life, the soul takes with it the
"treasure in heaven" created by the loving works we did in our
lives and also drags the chains we forged of selfishness. These
results and products—for good or for ill—are the creations of the
mind.

Furthering the idea of our triune nature, the Cayce readings
identify three levels of consciousness: the conscious, the subconscious, and the superconscious.

***The active principle that governs man. Mind* a factor, as the
senses are of the mind, and as the soul and spirit are factors of
the entity, one in all, all in one . . . The mind may be classified
into the two forces—that between the physical and soul, and
that between the soul and spirit force. We see the manifesta-**

tions of this, rather than the object or the mind itself. We find this always manifested through one of the senses, the same as we find the psychic forces a manifestation of the soul and spirit; the *mind* a manifestation of the physical. (3744-2)

Reading 3744-2 has more to say about the dynamic inter-workings between the part of the mind that our personalities use and the part of the mind that is in contact with the Universal Consciousness:

Definition of the words "conscious mind": The *conscious* means *that* that is able to be manifested in the physical plane through one of the senses.

Definition of the word "subconscious mind": That lying between the soul and spirit forces within the entity, and is reached more thoroughly when the conscious mind is under subjugation of the soul forces of the individual or physical body. We may see manifestation in those of the so-called spiritual minded people. The manifestation of the subconscious in their action. (3744-2)

Of course, the quality of what we create has everything to do with the quality of the life we are living. Even illness in the physical body is a result of "dis-ease" in the mind created by the misuse of spiritual forces for selfish thought and activity. These mistakes are the results of our choices, not those of God, for we determine how we will use the Creative Forces and thereby shape our personalities. Cayce explained the personality in this way: "There is the physical body, there is the mental body, there is the soul body. They are One, as the Trinity; yet these may find a manner of expression that is individual unto themselves. The body itself finds its own level in its *own* development." (281-24)

That which a conscious mind does with pleasure becomes a part of the entity's personality. Then, the natural question in gaining an appreciation of that which may be helpful in the developing of a soul-entity would be, what is [the] personality of a soul? The understanding of a body in the material environs as to the laws of a particular experience, making for that termed as sincerity of the entity, of the soul, pertaining to the law that is known, is the soul's personality. Think on that! (378-14)

The first sentence of this quotation bears repeating: *"That which a conscious mind does with pleasure becomes a part of the entity's personality."* It should seem an exciting discovery, then, that we can begin placing our love for God and love for each other high on our list of life's pleasures! We can allow the sheer *wanting* of oneness to be *fun*, in and of itself. Because mind is the builder, this choice would be to good effect.

The readings are generous with helpful teachings that can show us how the mind can help us rediscover oneness. Read the difference between soul and spirit, and the golden thread to oneness begins to lead us home within:

The soul is an individual, individuality, that may grow to be one with, or separate from, the whole. The spirit is the impelling influence of infinity, or the one creative source, force, that is manifest. Hence we find that in the physical plane we seek soul manifestation as the spirit moves same in activity. (5749-3)

Finally, the Cayce readings bring our potential into the light, by explaining the direct connection between consciousness and oneness, revealing that oneness links soul and spirit:

(Q) Explain what the divide between the soul and spiritual forces is. How manifest, and how we may study self to gain the approach to that divide.

(A) This [is] of the spiritual entity in its entirety. The superconscious [is] the divide, that one-ness lying between the soul and the spirit force, within the spiritual entity. Not of earth forces at all, only awakened with the spiritual indwelling and acquired individually. (900-21)

The next chapter explains some exciting ways in which we can navigate the sea of our thoughts, feelings, and desires, and find Universal Consciousness within—our direct connection to the superconscious mind of God. All it takes to get started is an honest desire to know God. This will bring the universal into the subconscious and from the subconscious into your conscious daily life.

(Q) Is it correct . . . that the superconsciousness is the mind or supreme controlling force of the Universal Forces?

(A) As pertaining to an individual, yes. As pertaining to Universal Forces, in the larger sense, no, but through the superconscious the Universal Forces are made active in subconsciousness. (900-31)

In the same reading we receive insights as to how the Universal Consciousness filters through to us, from the superconscious (God) to the human subconscious, in the example of Saul. Remember that mind is the builder. The mind of God gives and gives and gives, if we would but desire to receive. Once we receive and remember oneness, there is no limit to what we, too, can build:

(Q) Explain and illustrate the difference in the faculties of Mind, Subconscious and Superconscious.

(A) The superconscious mind being that of the spiritual entity, and in action only when the subconscious is become the conscious mind ... Illustrated, as has been given, in the light as came to Saul on way to Damascus. The superconsciousness of Jesus came to the subconscious of Saul, yet he could not retain in conscious that necessary for him to do. The superconscious came to that of him directed to act in the conscious manner, or Saul, as he continued in the subconscious, seeking for the light of that he could not make clear to his consciousness. (900-31)

In his book, Bucke relates the case of an individual who had a transforming religious experience, but who was not able to sustain the presence of the Universal Consciousness within him. "Here is a case of ascent into the full light of the morning before the actual rising of the sun," he writes. "This man was highly privileged, but it was not given to him to see 'the heavens opened.' He passed into the 'Brahmic Bliss,' but did not see the 'Brahmic Splendor.'"

In the next chapter, we will discover ways by which we can learn to bask in the sun that never sets.

EXPERIENCING THE ONENESS OF IT ALL

Think of your experience of oneness as a reality that you can gradually uncover within yourself through meditation. Each day use a concept from the following list as a focus, and try to observe it at work in the world around you. Try to be aware of how all things are connected, and feel your oneness with all life.

1. All souls are one, regardless of our individualized personalities. We were created at the same time, and we are equal in spirit. Even though the body wears out, we will never die.
2. All consciousness is contained in God Consciousness. Through our choices, we use our consciousness to either separate further from God or to join with God through loving words, thoughts, and deeds.
3. All love is one. Every loving word, thought, or deed joins with the oneness of God which is love.
4. All life is one: microbe, insect, plant, tree, bird, animal, human. Life is all one force.
5. My heart beats in the sound and rhythm of Om, and my breath is one with the expanding and contracting universe.
6. All forces are one force: attraction, repulsion; gravity, thrust, implosion, explosion, manifestation, pressure, heat, cold, light.
7. All that is manifest and unmanifest is vibration. All consciousness is vibration.
8. All emanations are one emanation: cosmic rays, radiation, fragrances, sound, love.
9. All geometry is one: the Great Pyramid, the fullness of space, the mind.
10. $E=mc^2$: energy and matter are one.
11. Every thought, word, and deed can be traced back to the beginning.
12. Christ Consciousness is within me and shows itself whenever I perform loving acts.

Chapter 6

TIME TO REMEMBER

IT WAS THERE ALL ALONG

On April 19, 1995, a powerful explosion rocked the Alfred C. Murrah Federal Building in Oklahoma City, ripping it to pieces and killing 168 people. Media reports came sporadically at first, as reporters tried to piece together the sketchy information. In disbelief, we viewed the obscene devastation on our TV screens and learned that the killing had been intentional. As a nation, we were galvanized by anger, even while moved with helpless compassion for the victims and their families.

On occasions such as this, time stops. All personal urgency is suspended. Concerns vanish. Our oneness as a nation also manifested during the 1986 Challenger disaster, when we were one in our grief over the loss of seven astronauts; a schoolteacher, Christa McAuliffe, among them. We were one in our breathless dread of nuclear catastrophe, as we watched the scud missiles nose-dive into Tel Aviv during the Persian Gulf War in 1991.

We are one, deep within our conscious minds, in our helplessness about plane crashes that are never solved, a figure skater whose knee is bludgeoned before a competition, and highly visible crimes for which no one seems to pay a serious penalty. We were inspired together when actor Bill Cosby, a grieving father, demonstrated before the world that love would prevail in his heart after the senseless murder of his son. Shootings now affect the rich and the poor alike, black or white, famous or unknown, adults, babies—there no longer seems to be a pattern for violence.

We are never really without our oneness with each other and

our oneness with God. Unfortunately, we usually don't demonstrate it except during such gut-wrenching situations. Behind it all, however, is the oneness of love, freedom, enjoyment of happiness, falling in and out of love, friendship, empathy, and gratitude that we all visit when joy makes us feel oneness—"together"—within ourselves. At one time or another, we may even be aware of it—for oneness is so close to the surface that it can eclipse all the clutter in our minds. As a nation, we beamed with pride at the safe return of the grinning Dr. Shannon Lucid from six months on the Russian space station, Mir. A place in the heart warms when we see the work of living saints and also when we see the heroism ordinary people demonstrate somewhere every day.

Like the sound of Om, our deeply vibrating oneness is always there, and it manifests even when no one notices. When the evidence of oneness is at its loudest, most of us don't recognize it for what it is—and that is our loss. We touch oneness as Christians at Christmas time, as Jews on Yom Kippur, as Muslims during the month of Ramadan, and Buddhists at Wesak. People of every path bow to oneness as we worship the Creator with whatever ember of sincerity may flicker in our hearts.

Beyond our sects, churches, and ideologies, we are one at the basic level of human experience. Our oneness as a race is apparent during disasters such as those mentioned above, but even without some visible tragedy or blessing to rivet our attention, as individuals we weave in and out of our chosen separation. We do this at those occasions when we feel gratitude beyond words; when devoting ourselves to another; while praying for something wonderful to come into our lives or praying that something painful be taken away—there is always someone, somewhere, praying. All prayer is one, and, as a reminder, we may revisit the words of Huston Smith that opened chapter 2:

What a strange fellowship this is. The God-seekers of every clime, lifting their voices in the most diverse ways imaginable to the God of all men. How does it all sound to Him? Like bedlam? Or, in some mysterious way, does it blend into harmony?

In the New Testament, Jesus tells us that the Kingdom of Heaven lies within us. He tells us that He was one with the Father in the beginning and that He is one with us. But, if the truth of our oneness lies within, how are we to find it? Can it be true that all mind is one—that all consciousness is the same force, the same energy focused differently through the kaleidoscope of human desires?

Not only can we remember oneness, say the readings, we can become one with the Universal Consciousness and change our lives for the better. We can get back on the divine track, and we don't have to stop having fun either. "Ask, and it will be given you; seek, and you will find; knock, and it will be opened to you." (Matthew 7:7) Cayce explained this most deep truth in another way, "And all that we may know of a universal consciousness is already within self." (3004-1)

It was there all along. All that remains for us now is taking a look inside and discovering the tools by which we can explore oneness on our own, for:

Thy body is indeed the temple of the living God. There He hath promised to meet thee. There He does commune with those that seek within the holy of holies. (2787-1)

"KNOW THYSELF"

Hugh Lynn Cayce's groundbreaking book, *Venture Inward*, helped introduce to Western people the idea known in the East for millennia, that turning within is the way to learn about human nature and to discover our oneness with God. The very name of God, I AM THAT I AM, revealed to Moses on Mt. Sinai, is the universal emblem of our divine being—of our oneness with God.

I AM. I AM. I AM.

As we say these words, we call ourselves by the name of God. We call ourselves by the name of that which is permanent, divine, all-encompassing love. We are one with God. One with each other, whenever we call out this name.

We have followed our connection to I AM THAT I AM from Moses back through the centuries, tracing it through ancient Egypt and on through ancient texts from around the world. We then followed the golden thread by way of the Edgar Cayce readings to the beginning of creation. We shall now "venture inward" and discover oneness for ourselves.

The ancient Greeks had inscribed "Know thyself" on the walls of the temple at Delphi. Oedipus, Socrates, and many others had sought counsel there, but Socrates was unconvinced that "knowing self" was possible. In chapter 3, the strong connection be-

tween the early Greek philosophers and the Egyptian mystery
theology at Heliopolis led us to Plato's account of Atlantis.
Socrates, an old friend of Plato's family, was also a close friend of
Critias, who, you will remember, told Plato the Atlantis story.
Ironically, Socrates was poisoned in 399 B.C. for the heresy of
insisting that the Sophists make their arguments more scientific.

The ideas of Socrates and others strongly influenced the Age
of Enlightenment with the apotheosis of the scientific method.
Socrates fought against the principle of "know thyself," because
he concluded that only observable knowledge is dependable—
and that you cannot know an inner self because there is nothing
outward to observe. The Cayce readings, of course, disagree on
this point. "First, analyze thyself," says reading 3004-1. "Know
thyself, for he indeed that knows himself knows his God also. And
be sure ye know what and who is, and where is, thy God. These
must be answered within self." (3004-1)

The idea of looking within, of studying the geometry of the
inner self as a mini-universe or microcosm of the whole of God,
grew out of the mystery religion traditions. The mystery religions
emerged in ancient Greece as disparate "cults," but the threads
of truth that they contained are traceable to early Christian, Buddhist, Vedic, and Egyptian origins. From the mystery religions
came Gnosticism, which means "knowing." (Agnostic means
"unknowing.") In her book *The Gnostic Gospels*, Elaine Pagels
explains the fundamental principle of Gnosticism: "Yet to know
oneself, at the deepest level, is simultaneously to know God; this
is the secret of *gnosis*."

It is important to understand this statement correctly, for
when viewed from the outside looking in, it would appear to suggest a form of narcissism. When viewed from the inside outward,
however, we find that it is possible—and not all that difficult, if
we are willing to simplify our thinking—to discover divine reality within us, for our observation, our comfort, and our delight.

A simple practice of meditation, as well as a healthy desire to
discover God's true and perfect flame in our hearts, will help us
identify and avoid the artificial thoughts and feelings that obscure our knowledge of oneness. Meditation practice can also
help us identify in the outside world that which is not of God and
live our lives more wisely.

**As Moses gave of old, it isn't who will descend from heaven to
bring you a message, nor who would come from over the seas,**

but lo, ye find Him within thine own heart, within thine own consciousness! If ye will *meditate,* open thy heart, thy mind! Let thy body and mind be channels, that *ye* may *do* the things ye ask God to do for you! Thus ye come to know Him. (281-41)

MINDFULNESS AND THE GOLDEN PRESENT

Westerners tend to have difficulty slowing down, quieting, and focusing the mind in meditation, and there are two reasons for this. We are tugged this way and that by all the externals of the world and we are also drawn to where our desires lure us. We get lazy and millions actually look to the shouting imagery and seductive sounds, to the machines, the computers, appliances, and gadgets to make us happy. We are sometimes so paranoid about what has already happened in our lives and fearful of what is about to happen that we can literally spend years without actually "being in the moment"—which is really all we have. Just the present. The constant present. The now. And we lose the *now,* even now—slipping away, instant by instant—whether we are in the present or lost in the past or that which has not yet happened.

Eastern teachers over the years have traveled as amazed missionaries to teach neurotic Westerners what is so obvious—simply how to relax and capture the present moment in order to be happy. They see us as lost in our materialism to the point where the mind has no discipline, and fears, stress, and ambition drive us. Swami Satchidananda teaches that the "golden present" is all that exists: the past is gone and the future hasn't happened yet. Opportunity exists only in the *now.*

Vietnamese Buddhist Zen master Thich Nhat Hanh teaches "mindfulness," a call to be mindfully present in everything we do, not scattered in thought or worry, but concentrating, enjoying, loving what we do, moment by moment. He teaches that, yes, we need to plan, but to be free in the moment, even if planning is what is taking place. Once planned, remain in the moment as you go about your day.

"The Buddha once said that the problem of life and death is itself the problem of mindfulness," writes Hanh in his book, *The Miracle of Mindfulness.* "Whether or not one is alive, depends on whether one is mindful."

The idea of mindfulness is easy to grasp. "Wash the dishes to wash the dishes," he writes, "not for the cup of tea afterwards." This should be our attitude, no matter what we are doing. Be in the moment. Enjoy the peace of each thing you do and think about nothing else: washing your hands, sweeping the floor, drinking your coffee. "Chopping wood is meditation. Carrying water is meditation. Be mindful twenty-four hours a day." By practicing this conscientious attitude, we can quiet ourselves from within and begin our approach to the Universal Consciousness.

These keys to breaking our modern habits of distraction, worry, and stress will go a long way in helping us learn a basic meditation in which we can feel our divine oneness more intently. There are many styles and techniques of meditation used the world over and presenting even a brief overview of them would be beyond the scope of this book. Instead, it offers a practice that is easy to learn and remember and that can be used anytime to contemplate your oneness with the universe. First, however, let us see what meditation is and how it can help us.

In their book, *Meditation and the Mind of Man*, authors Herbert B. Puryear and Mark Thurston state that "The invitation to the Comforter [Holy Spirit] to come is the spirit of meditation!" The prophets, great and minor, practiced meditation: Moses on the mount; Samuel in his closet; David in the cave; and the Master Himself in the desert and in the garden. In these places they all received communications from God of weighty issues pertaining to their lives, the future of their people, and the fulfillment of the divine plan on earth.

The fact is, the Cayce readings encourage us to practice a style of meditation based on the way in which *Jesus Himself* taught meditation. *Meditation and the Mind of Man* is one of the finest books on meditation for Westerners who wish to learn how to go within, for it concisely explains the techniques and the benefits as well.

"Of the many benefits of meditation," write the authors, "the Cayce readings promise that it can make one stronger, physically, mentally, emotionally, and spiritually, and consequently more able to be of help to others."

The basics provided here will help anyone accomplish his or her desire to realize the oneness of life, God, and love by regularly spending some "quality time" with the Universal Consciousness. It's time that we do, for "Deep within us is our true nature," as author and speaker John Van Auken writes in his book *Spiritual Breakthrough*. "Deep within us, we remember the original home, and we know the way. Each of us was there in the beginning. Each of us was originally created within the image and likeness of God. Within us that original nature lives and intuitively knows its way home."

It is time for us to do this, for it was prophesied in Malachi and Joel:

... put me to the test, says the LORD of hosts, if I will not open the windows of heaven for you and pour down for you an overflowing blessing. (Malachi 3:10)

And it shall come to pass afterward, that I will pour out my spirit on all flesh; your sons and your daughters shall prophesy, your old men shall dream dreams, and your young men shall see visions. (Joel 2:28)

The Edgar Cayce readings state that "*Meditation is emptying* self of all that hinders the creative forces from rising along the natural channels of the physical man ... " (281-13) At first, "emptying self" sounds like a mysterious Zen koan, because all you know about *you* seems to be *there* at all times. However, you will soon discover a quiet room in your soul which exists behind all the noise. This is a level of your consciousness which is already very close to the Universal Consciousness, *even as you read this.*

The Edgar Cayce readings have helped many thousands of people learn to meditate. Here is one of the most cogent passages:

(Q) Please advise me about my meditations.

(A) First study to know what meditation is. As has been indicated; the relationships first of body, mind, soul; then as these are understood, the *natural* forces, the *natural* manners of meditation will become as a part of self. Read oft those things that are promises as are given in the New Testament. Learn those by heart, not as rote but read them to know how they apply to self. And you will have meditation. (308-3)

"When we find the Bible, Edgar Cayce, Tibetan Buddhism, and ancient Taoism in agreement on so many principles," writes Puryear in the Preface to *Meditation and the Mind of Man*, "we may sense a discovery of universal laws; for example, all of these sources emphasize the importance of the mind, and none of them promises an easy way."

From this point of view, we can pick up some handy tips that will help us when we first practice to commune with oneness—and bring its benefits into our lives.

CALM ABIDING

Meditation is extremely important for helping us sort out our thoughts and feelings and be able to hear God speaking to us in the language of the Universal Consciousness: love, guidance, patience, healing, freedom, peace.

In his book, *The Second Coming*, author Kirk Nelson states that "The use of meditation and spiritual living quickens the body of matter to the level of energy, and beyond to the universal consciousness." As you practice the meditation exercise below, remember that the deepest part of you is already one with Christ and you never stopped being one with that Christ.

. . . all knowledge that ye may have is within self. For, thy body, thy mind, thy soul, is a part of that universal consciousness. Thus ye become aware of same. But know, the application of same is not to the glory of self, but to Him, who is the Way, the Truth and the Light. (2981-1)

The ancient practice of Tibetan meditation is designed to return our inner environment to the clean, clear pristine state that it was in the beginning. It is one of the most complete and thorough meditation systems on earth. Buddhists and meditation students spend lifetimes perfecting its techniques—unlike Western psychology, it thoroughly comprehends all the complexities of the mind—works to clear the landscape of mental development from the jungle of our afflictions. Identifying our unhappiness as having arisen from our attachments to the Desire Realm, meditation clears us by building on the hidden potentials for change that eagerly await within us: stability, clarity, and calm.

The goals of Tibetan meditation from this point of view work hand-in-hand with the recommendations of the Cayce readings. These goals are (1) "calm abiding" and (2) a sense of "special insight" which is the result.

> Knowing that special insight endowed with calm
>   abiding
> Thoroughly destroys the afflictive emotions,
> One must initially seek calm abiding.

It is achieved by those liking nonattachment to the
world.
　　　　　—Bodhisattva Shantideva
　　　　　Engaging in the Bodhisattva Deeds, VIII, 4

As Cayce instructed, we must approach meditation with a
clean heart and mind. We can expect the special insight in the
form of guidance from God—"ask, and it will be given you."
Naturally, if you sit down hoping to contact the Universal
Consciousness and you bring negative feelings with you,
nonvirtuous desires, and selfish motives, the Universal Consciousness will flee—self-aggrandizement is what created the
separation from it in the first place! A sense of givingness and
the quality of love are the only required tolls at the gates of the
Universal Consciousness. The strength of our urges to keep ourselves separated will determine how easy or difficult this process will be.

**Will ye make thy will one with the Creative Force? Or will ye
be negligent or unmindful of thy opportunities, or will ye rebel
and have thine own way? (3376-2)**

Whether meditation comes easily or with difficulty, whenever
one chooses to turn away from the self and align with God, the
process requires patience. Perfecting it lasts a lifetime—and even
many lifetimes. The idea of "calm abiding," therefore, should be
practiced all day every day, like purity of heart, kindness, and
nonharmfulness to all. Hoping to clear the continuous habits of
years from a carnal jungle two brief minutes before meditation,
however, can't guarantee an ideal meditation environment. The
desire to align with oneness must be full-time. In chapter 1, we
read Cayce's advice to stockbroker Morton Blumenthal to spend
"six months" on his first lesson (900-429). Six months, therefore,
is a worthy goal.

The readings advise each person to find his or her own best
way to meditate and not to compare results with others. They
also offer guidelines on how to get started. If prayer is talking to
God, meditation is listening for the answer, but you need to quiet
your mind and practice in order to achieve results. Empty yourself of separating desires, distractions, expectations, and be
clean of heart and mind.

**In whatever manner that thine own consciousness is a
cleansing of the body and of the mind, that ye may present thy-**

self *clean* before thyself and before thy God, *do!* Whether washing of the body with water, purging of same with oils, or surrounding same with music or incense. But *do that thy consciousness* directs thee! Not questioning! For he that doubteth has already built his barrier! (826-11)

We have to do more than *desire* to know oneness. We also need to *manifest a belief* in our oneness through our commitment to finding God within. We do this through the action of a brief daily practice of meditation and through God's grace. Approach meditation with gratitude, therefore, and be open to the Universal Consciousness to guide you from within:

Find that which is to *yourself* the more certain way to your consciousness of *purifying* body and mind, before ye attempt to enter into the meditation as to raise the image of that through which ye are seeking to know the will or the activity of the Creative Forces, for ye are *raising* in meditation actual *creation* taking place within the inner self! (281-13)

The Cayce readings recommend that, prior to meditation, people dedicate themselves to divine purpose. This is to establish a suitable attitude and mental environment, as well as to reinforce a sense of protection for your thought processes. It is best done verbally, by aligning yourself with the Universal Consciousness through a brief prayer. Before you pray, visualize yourself being surrounded with white light and say:

Here am I, O God, use me—send me! Do with me as Thou seest! Not my will, but Thine—O God—be done in and through me. (826-11)

With practice, you will discover that the state of meditation creates a peaceful improvement in your normal state of mind. If you have ever allowed your mind to wander peacefully while you were driving long distances or mowing the lawn, you have visited that state without knowing it. The tips on meditation below will guide you. Practice them once or twice, and you will remember them and be able to use them for the rest of your life.

Prepare for Meditation

- Set a special time each day for meditation.
- Try to use the same quiet, secluded place each day.
- Sit in a comfortable, straight-backed chair. (Use yogic postures if you prefer, but it is better not to lie down.)

- Close your eyes and take three slow deep breaths through the nose, releasing them through the mouth. The inbreath and outbreath reflect the expansion and contraction of the universe.
- Consciously relax the body from toes to the head, releasing the tension in all muscles.
- Leave all worries and concerns outside your meditation space. Think of this time and place as sacred.
- Don't fall asleep, but just enjoy the quiet and the knowledge that you want to be aware of your oneness.
- You may use incense and soft, meditative music, if you wish.
- Don't expect results, but invite the Universal Consciousness—God—to guide you with grace.

Once you close your eyes and relax, invite the good feeling of peace to fill you. It's like the new feeling that you have when you first discover that someone is in love with you, only in this case it is God. This state arises out of that peaceful place that you prepare within and that you visit regularly by keeping "self first in that attitude and purpose of a universal consciousness for the good of all." (3184-1) Practice. Visualize the beauty of oneness in all things. Go into meditation every day with faith and don't expect results, sensations, merit badges—avoid putting pressure on yourself, because this is the place where you can enjoy freedom from pressure of any kind. This is where you "trust" and have "faith" that the unseen Universal Consciousness will manifest within you as joy and healing.

Once you have prepared for meditation, distracting thoughts will come, even distractions from the outside. When they do, simply bless them and send them on their way—don't let them take you with them. Should you remember that you left the stove on—by all means, get up and turn it off! However, unless the thought is practical and urgent, during this precious, peaceful time in which you come to God "face to face," protect the place you create for meditation and return there often as your daily, peaceful treat and retreat. Practice being the observer in this way and open the door to higher consciousness. Eventually, you will realize that God will reveal the fundamental oneness of our existence, the I AM presence of our awareness.

GO ON UP AND TALK TO GOD

The following steps are for preparing to talk to God in your own language, and listening for God to talk back to you in divine language. Do this by the "closing of self to the physical consciousness, and letting the universal consciousness flow through thy mind, thy body, thy soul; surrounding self with the awareness of His abiding presence with thee, ever." (967-3) You will learn to anticipate the quiet moments of relaxation and find that they reduce stress and give you a boost of energy. Once you have relaxed your entire body, follow these steps using the affirmations from the Temple Beautiful (the complete list, from reading 281-25, can be found at the end of chapter 4). Jotting them onto small cards and holding them in your hands will help you.

A Meditation for Experiencing Oneness

- Feel your oneness with all that is God. Believe it. Assume it.

Affirm: LORD, THE MAKER OF HEAVEN AND EARTH, THE GIVER OF THE CHRIST IN THE HEARTS OF MEN, QUICKEN THOU THE SPIRIT WITHIN, THAT THY LIGHT, THY LOVE, MAY BE MANIFESTED THROUGH ME.

- Feel your oneness with all the best in yourself and your neighbors. Believe it. Assume it.

Affirm: LORD, THOU ART MY DWELLING PLACE. ABIDE THOU, O GOD, IN THE TEMPLE OF MY BODY, THAT IT MAY BE WHOLLY AS THOU WOULD HAVE IT.

- Ask God to shed grace upon your consciousness and awareness, for understanding and spiritual growth. Believe it. Assume it.

Affirm: LORD, THOU ART MY DWELLING PLACE. QUICKEN THE SPIRIT WITHIN ME THAT THOU MAY HAVE THY WAY WITH ME, THAT I MAY BE THE GREATER CHANNEL OF BLESSINGS TO OTHERS.

- Feel love for all and know that this feeling is bringing into manifestation the oneness that we knew, in the beginning, before the world was made.

- Try to remain silently at-one for a minimum of three minutes, or for as long as you like.

- Verbalize your commitment to heal the choices by which you separated from the One. Use this closing affirmation:

Affirm: LORD, LEAD THOU THE WAY. I COMMIT MY BODY, MY MIND, TO BE ONE WITH THEE.

Go on up and talk to God at least once, if not three times, every day for six months. Practice feeling your oneness with the Creator and manifesting love for others—practice *being* the "Firstborn" within you. The Universal Consciousness will do the rest, if you but have faith in the "conviction of things not seen."

If you have difficulties with meditation at first, it will help to think of the mind as an untrained puppy. First you must leash it. Then teach it to be calm and not dart all over. Eastern traditions teach meditators how to do this by learning how to be the passive *observer* of your thoughts, rather than the active *thinker*. This is because, even without your thoughts, you still exist. You know that consciousness does not end when you go to sleep. Neither does it end when you cease "thinking" and enter meditation. Allow thoughts to pass by like clouds across the sky, and don't let them seduce you. Let nothing distract you from oneness when you are in your sacred meditation space.

The Edgar Cayce readings advise people to practice yogic breathing and to use affirmations or mantras (sacred sounds). He suggested, for example, the use of humming or chants to help attune the vibrations of body, mind, and spirit, and focus concentration inward. In reading 2823-3 he suggested the syllables: *o-o-o-ah-ah-umm-o-o-o*. You can, of course, also use Om, I AM THAT I AM, or a host of others from various traditions.

When you begin your period of regular meditations, work at keeping your mind and heart clean of ill-will or those familiar desires that you know are not good for you. With practice, you will be able to attune your mind, and you will gradually rise in spirit according to the pace that the Universal Consciousness will set for you. Your deeper and deeper sense of closeness to oneness will grow stronger by the day, as you show yourself attuning to the divine through ethical thought and action. Above all, have faith that God wants to talk to you as much as you want to talk with God, so keep your mind free of doubts. Remember that self-condemnation is one of our biggest stumbling blocks:

Then, know thy ideal. Apply same—studying to show self approved unto that ideal which thou may set in thy activities; keeping self from condemnation—which has at times brought and does bring such a fear of showing self worthy. (2170-1)

In his book, *Spiritual Breakthrough*, author and speaker John Van Auken points out that "We must drive out of our minds this accuser, this self-doubt, this self-condemning influence, if we are to fully regain God-consciousness. Our consciousness will rejoice when it is done . . . "

Here, the Edgar Cayce readings describe the beauty of the inner experience, a visit with quiet joy to which we are all entitled as often as we wish:

. . . *in* meditation . . . that *healing of every* kind and nature may be disseminated on the wings of thought . . . Then, either with the aid of a low music, or the incantation [mantra] of that which carries self deeper—deeper—to the seeing, feeling, experiencing of that image in the creative forces of love, enter into the Holy of Holies. As self feels or experiences the raising of this, see it disseminated through the *inner* eye (not the carnal eye) to that which will bring the greater understanding in meeting every condition in the experience of the body. Then listen to the music that is made as each center of thine own body responds to that new creative force that little by little this entering in will enable self to renew all that is necessary—in Him. (281-13)

If you find yourself "struggling" during meditation, you are more than likely allowing your *expectations* to be your focus! Beginners, especially, tend to make unnecessary complications and start meditation practice with anxious expectation. This is to be avoided. God does not want you to be anxious! Just relax and give God the opportunity to manifest in your mind.

Even though one can spend a lifetime perfecting meditation work, it's as simple as this to get started incorporating oneness into your experiences, views, and attitudes. These basic principles are enough to give you a map, a goal, a simple practice to follow, in order to approach the gate to oneness a few times each day. The rest is up to your persistence in knowing God in your life and trusting the Universal Consciousness to lead you through those gates.

The idea of our oneness is conveyed in the most unexpected places, and you should notice the truth of oneness often during the day. Find new oneness ideas to focus on during meditation, and that way you can keep your meditations fresh. New ideas are everywhere! For example, following is a poem about how we are one with the food we eat—one with the earth and one with the Creator:

> The very spot where grew the bread
> That formed my bones, I see.
> How strange, old field, on thee to tread
> And feel I'm part of thee.

The sentiment of oneness in this poem can be found in Buddhism, Hinduism, Islam, Judaism, and Christianity. It is a mere bite into the apple of oneness. However, the point did not escape its author, Abraham Lincoln. The Cayce readings put it this way:

For within the human body—living, not dead—*living* human forces—we find every element, every gas, every mineral, every influence that is outside of the organism itself. For indeed it is one with the whole. (470-22)

As you meditate, thank God for interruptions and bless those who interrupt you, for each one is an opportunity for you to learn to love. But limit diversions and disturbing thoughts so that your senses can practice stillness. Also, use what Edgar Cayce termed an "ideal." Use a high ideal to guide your life, and use it in meditation as well.

Then, meditate upon that which is thy highest ideal within thyself, raise the vibrations from thy lower self, thy lower consciousness through the centers of thy body to the temple of thy mind, thy brain, thy eye that is single in purpose; or to the glandular forces of the body as the Single Eye. Then, listen—listen! For it is not in the storm, not in the noise, but the still small voice that rises within. (826-11)

Of ideals, Cayce said, "Ideas and ideals are quite different. One arises from the infinite, the other from the finite." (3211-2) Let rediscovering your oneness with God, with Creation, and with the Christ be your Ideal as you practice meditating. And, as you periodically reread this book, let the journey be your guide.

Give yourself the opportunity to spend entire days being mindful and looking for the oneness of the universe and your oneness with it. Think of all people as being one in the bosom of the lightning bolt of creative love by which we were brought into self-awareness. This will be your key to discovering oneness in your life and helping you live your life differently from now on— not as a separate entity trying to find your way back to God, but by recognizing immediately that you never really left. All you have to do is heal the separation you chose when you made yourself, your problems, your desires, more important than your oneness with God.

SEED THOUGHTS ON
THE UNIVERSAL CONSCIOUSNESS

Use these seed thoughts when you meditate. You can put each one on a card in your meditation space, and read it before closing your eyes.

. . . each soul is in that consciousness it has builded—by what it has done *about* Universal Consciousness in its experiences. (2390-7)

Then the judgment, then the ideal, is that of the universal love, Universal Consciousness—that as was and is, and ever will be, manifest in Him, even the Christ—as was shown in the flesh in the *man* called Jesus! (954-5)

. . . what *is* ideal or what *is* the ideal? In the term or sense indicated here, ideal means spiritual things, mental things, material things that are constructive in their nature, or that produce within the experience of the entity a greater awareness with the Universal Consciousness . . . (2554-1)

This is the nearest representation of that to which each soul seeks to attain, to be one with the Universal Consciousness and yet aware of itself. This ye alone can attain, in making the ideal that as was manifested by Him, who is the way. (5106-1)

For each soul enters for a purposefulness, that it may be a channel through which this Universal Consciousness—that is ever present, and being sought as it were by the inmost forces of the entity—may be seen, may find expression in the experience of the fellow man. (1297-1)

Hence we find that as an individual entity minimizes the faults, magnifies the virtues, the soul-entity grows more and more in the awareness of that consciousness which is to the entity ideal. (2554-1)

Chapter 7

LOVE STORY

ANKLE DEEP IN ONENESS

Morton Blumenthal, the stockbroker who was introduced at the beginning of chapter 1, asked many questions of Cayce in the 468 readings that he received. Like others who found Cayce's advice difficult to practice, he occasionally repeated his questions. Cayce's response to those who would ask questions for a second or third time was often " . . . as given" or "Review that already given." Ever compassionate and patient with his questioners, the source would, nevertheless, try to rephrase the lesson in order to help the questioner "get it."

In God's every attempt to break through the veil of humankind's self-chosen exile from oneness, we have tended to struggle over and over again with the same problems and lessons of remembering our oneness and practicing it. We have been given laws, rules, guidelines, reasons to know why certain choices will lead to misery, and why other choices will lead to our ultimate joy and knowledge of eternal life. We've been given saints who have demonstrated the Universal Consciousness and scholars who have given us helpful commentaries on God's Word.

During an earlier reading, Blumenthal had questioned what it is that now separates the soul from the spiritual forces and how we can bridge that separation and rejoin the oneness. The answer moves us swiftly to the conclusion that it all hangs on how we conduct our lives, how we think, live, how we practice what we believe, and how we apply our ideals in every aspect of our lives. As a bonus, say the readings, the Creator wants to make oneness part of our manifest reality once again:

Study to show thyself approved unto Him, rightly dividing the words of truth, keeping self unspotted from the world, avoiding the appearance of evil, for as is given, those who would seek God must believe that He IS, and a rewarder of those who would seek Him. That is, that *the Creator has that One-ness with the individual to make that One-ness with Him.* As is given in the conditions as is manifest through those who would seek the One-ness with God, for only those who have approached sufficient to make the mind of the physical, the mind of the soul, the mind of the spiritual, One with Him, may understand or gather that necessary to approach that understanding. (900-21) [italics added]

We can help to eliminate our condition of separation by realizing that God is unchanging, whole, patient, available, whenever we get tired of trying to be our own individual, arrogant little universes. It is up to us as individuals to make the effort. "Success will come about," states mystical writer Joel S. Goldsmith, in his book *Consciousness Unfolding,* "in proportion as you attain some measure of spiritual consciousness."

The Cayce readings advise us to take action with a sincere heart, because the joy we seek is within us:

How sincere *is* the *desire* on the part of each *to* know The Lord Thy God Is One? Sufficient to be active rather than just passive in the statement? For, he that would gain the concept must believe that He is; and that He rewards those who seek to do His biddings. Then, let each be active; up and doing, with a heart that is singing the joyous message that the Kingdom of Heaven is at hand. It *is* within! I *am* the brother! I *am* the associate with the Son, in the relationships to the Father! (262-42)

In manifesting our conscious connection to our oneness, we mustn't think like a child who dips his toe into the water to see if it is too cold. After all, the endless ocean of infinite oneness is our natural home, and we're already ankle deep. It surrounds us always and forever. It is our destination, because it was our origin, except that, as we consciously chose to separate, we must return as a result of that same conscious choosing. It can only help us to acknowledge and seek the consciousness that says, *I am one with God,* and all our choices, from that moment on, will become clearer and easier to judge.

Take the plunge of faith into oneness by first assuming it, and do not let fear of failure play a part.

CHRIST CONSCIOUSNESS

"Let thine eye be single," as you seek the oneness within, and the journey will be that much shorter. This means that we need to demonstrate oneness in our thoughts, words, and actions, but without also demonstrating contradictions.

For where your treasure is, there will your heart be also. The eye is the lamp of the body. So, if your eye is sound, your whole body will be full of light; but if your eye is not sound, your whole body will be full of darkness. If then the light in you is darkness, how great is the darkness! (Matthew 6:21-23)

The quotation from Matthew continues with the enjoinder to guard against letting our light be darkness (consciousness that is disconnected from Christ Consciousness). It says that we simply cannot serve two masters—The Lord thy God, after all, is One.

Goldsmith writes, "Spiritual consciousness is that state of consciousness from which world beliefs have disappeared in some measure. Spiritual consciousness, or Christ consciousness, is that state of consciousness which no longer reacts to things in the outer realm. You are infinite, spiritual consciousness. You are the law unto your own experience." This is the element of free will, about which the Cayce readings have much to say. However, this quotation from reading 329-1 will serve us well:

But, it should be remembered by every soul, there is no influence within the activities of an entity, a soul, that surpasses the *will* of self; the *will*, that may make one close in relationship to the Universal Consciousness, to the creative influences, or that may separate one from such influences. (329-1)

As we noted in chapter 4, reading 884-1 identified the Law of One as Christ Consciousness: " . . . the way of the Law of One—or that manifested in the present as the Christ Consciousness . . . " The Firstborn, Amilius, worked from the time of Adam to preserve the ancient teachings of prehistory so that we would remember what He, as the risen Jesus Christ, remembered from the beginning. He has preserved the records from Atlantis, the Ark of the Covenant, the Law and the Prophets, the birth and resurrection of Jesus of Nazareth, when He became the fully realized Christ. Universal Consciousness is the "fathomless totality" from which Christ spoke His parables and performed His miracles. He was ever one with that Universal Consciousness and one with the Father:

Father, I desire that they also, whom thou hast given me, may be with me where I am, to behold my glory which thou hast given me in thy love for me before the foundation of the world. (John 17:24)

In John 14:4, Jesus said, "And you know the way where I am going." We can rediscover our oneness with the Universal Consciousness and, yes, we already know the way. We can free ourselves once again to be one with the Christ Consciousness within, just as He did. The first twelve verses of John 14 actually comprise a beautiful love poem from the Firstborn, written to help us remember our access to oneness and the Universal Consciousness. The verses have been arranged in a list called "Christ's Keys to the Universal Consciousness," on the next page, for use in daily meditation. Try using them for a week or two, using each key on a subsequent day. As you do, simply let the Universal Consciousness do the teaching, as you master the universal law of "patience."

CHRIST'S KEYS TO THE
UNIVERSAL CONSCIOUSNESS

In John 14:1-12, Jesus answers the riddle of the trinity with the answer of oneness. Oneness is easy. Oneness is simple. The Christ and the Father are one. Christ is one with us, if we but choose to believe and to understand. Use these keys in a series of meditations.

1. "Let not your hearts be troubled; believe in God, believe also in me.

2. "In my Father's house are many rooms; if it were not so, would I have told you that I go to prepare a place for you?

3. "And when I go and prepare a place for you, I will come again and will take you to myself, that where I am you may be also.

4. "And you know the way where I am going."

5. Thomas said to him, "Lord, we do not know where you are going; how can we know the way?"

6. Jesus said to him, "I am the way, and the truth, and the life; no one comes to the Father, but by me.

7. "If you had known me, you would have known my Father also; henceforth you know him and have seen him."

8. Philip said to him, "Lord, show us the Father, and we shall be satisfied."

9. Jesus said to him, "Have I been with you so long, and yet you do not know me, Philip? He who has seen me has seen the Father; how can you say, 'Show us the Father'?

10. "Do you not believe that I am in the Father and the Father in me? The words that I say to you I do not speak on my own authority; but the Father who dwells in me does his works.

11. "Believe me that I am in the Father and the Father in me; or else believe me for the sake of the works themselves.

12. "Truly, truly, I say to you, he who believes in me will also do the works that I do; and greater works than these will he do, because I go to the Father."

Our innate knowledge of eternal life is a spark we have carried with us through every incarnation as the needle and thread of desire and karma pass in and out of the fabric of manifested reality. It is the soul, that Firstborn soul within us all, that eternal part of our consciousness which is ever one with eternity. It is our choice how much we allow that soul to drink of the Universal Consciousness exemplifying the Christ Consciousness in our daily lives.

He, that Christ Consciousness, is that first spoken of in the beginning when God said, "Let there be light, and there was light." And that is the light manifested in the Christ. First it became physically conscious in Adam. And as in Adam we all die, so in the last Adam—Jesus, becoming the Christ—we are all made alive. Not unto that as of one, then. For we each meet our own selves, even as He; though this did not become possible, practical in a world experience, until He, Jesus, became the Christ and made the way. (2879-1)

A great spiritual teacher of the nineteenth century commented on the deeply personal and intimate nature of the experience of the Universal Consciousness: "Bibles may convey and priests expound, but it is exclusively for the noiseless operation of one's isolated *Self* to enter the pure ether of veneration, reach the divine levels, and commune with the unutterable."

The teacher who wrote this was neither a Christian minister nor a yogi, not a Buddhist priest, and in fact never belonged to any church in his whole life. Yet, known for his pacifism and gentle wisdom, he helped us rid ourselves of the blight of slavery and heal the wounds of our most terrible war. In the passage above, from his *Democratic Vistas,* Walt Whitman speaks an eternal truth that has been uttered by every enlightened teacher the world has known, even by Jesus the Christ, who told us very simply that the Kingdom of Heaven lies within us.

THE SECOND COMING

We have never stopped being the children of God—the beautiful souls of light who originally beamed with an unwavering love, focused solely on the Creator. We are the ones who created separation and who now, through our increasing hunger for spiritual nourishment, seek to undo it. We firstly need to choose, as individuals, to stop believing that our separation from God is too difficult to change, and secondly to begin believing that God reaches out perpetually to awaken us and show us the path to the light.

Many believe that now is the time of the Second Coming of Christ—the manifested reality of Christ's message in John 14:1-12. His return is echoed in sources that include the biblical books of Daniel, the prophecies of Nostradamus, and the Edgar Cayce readings, which say that it will occur around 1998—the same period when the readings say that the preserved history and teachings of Atlantis would be found in the Hall of Records near the paws of the Great Sphinx.

The Second Coming is an important element in our understanding of ourselves, and our relationship to oneness and the Universal Consciousness—because, above all, I AM THAT I AM gives us extra help (grace) in this critical and wonderful period:

Then again He may come in body to claim His own. Is He abroad today in the earth? Yea, in those that cry unto Him from every corner; for He, the Father, hath not suffered His soul to see corruption; neither hath it taken hold on those things that make the soul afraid. For, He *is* the Son of Light, of God, and is holy before Him. And He comes again in the hearts and souls and minds of those that seek to know His ways. (5749-5)

The call to all people to turn inward and find their connection to oneness is an important part of our ability to recognize the long-awaited delivery of the Second Coming. Whether you believe that Jesus will literally return in the flesh or whether the Second Coming will be the awakening of the Universal Consciousness within—or both—doesn't much matter. The reason is because the artificial goblins of power and the distracting scenery of human creation with which we maintain our separation will certainly, inevitably, be burned away by the blinding arc-light of the Christ. Maintaining the Christ-connection in our conscious daily life merely requires that we incorporate the ideas, virtues, and love of God in our thoughts. Through diligence, we can practice the love of the Firstborn, as Jesus the Pattern demonstrated for us:

Or, as we have given as to how a soul becomes conscious, aware, of its contact with the universal-cosmic-God-Creative Forces in its experience; by feeding upon the food, the fruits, the results of spirit, of God, of Life, of Reality: love, hope, kindness, gentleness, brotherly love, patience. *These* make for the

awareness in the soul of its relationship to the Creative Force that is manifest in self, in the ego, in the I AM of each soul, and of I AM THAT I AM. (378-14)

"The purpose of this message is to set you free through a spiritual awareness of your oneness with God," writes Joel S. Goldsmith in *Consciousness Unfolding.* "If you find your oneness with God, you will need no contact with 'man, whose breath is in his nostrils.'" This is not to say that we do not need each other's help nor even that others can do our spiritual work for us. Each of us is responsible for making ourselves comfortable in the experience of oneness. As we do, as our determination peels back the bad habits of time, we will know the joy and freedom that the Universal Consciousness can reveal to us:

For it is in the application, not the knowledge, that the truth becomes a part of thee. It is not in thine body that what ye eat is thy body, but that the body—through thy digestive self—puts *into use in* muscle, bone, blood, tissue—yea the very blood and the very streams through which the mentality flows! Thy *brain* is not thy mind, it is that which is used by thy mind! (826-11)

Once your heart is full, your mind is at peace, and you see the light of the truth of oneness in the universe, all that you need to increase it is to transform knowledge into love and then share it with others. What could this be but fulfilling the words of Jesus who declared:

The first is, "Hear, O Israel: The Lord our God, the Lord is one; and you shall love the Lord your God with all your heart, and with all your soul, and with all your mind, and with all your strength." The second is this, "You shall love your neighbor as yourself." There is no other commandment greater than these. (Mark 12:29-31)

In terms of application, Cayce gives us practical suggestions. He was once asked:

(Q) Please give that which will be of help in my present development to attain the Christ Consciousness.

(A) Applying that—*applying* that—which has been so oft given. Let love direct thee, with little thought of self; rather with the attitude that the Christ Love, the Christ Consciousness may be made manifest day by day. (272-9)

Jesus Christ said that good acts, thoughts, and words that demonstrate love earn a permanent place in the soul's treasure box by which it will return to the perfect memory which is eternity.

In his insightful book, *The Second Coming of Christ*, Hindu teacher and author Paramahansa Yogananda throws yet another light on the process of our "remembering."

God did not reflect His pure Christ Intelligence in all matter in order to let it act like an eternal detective to punish man. This Christ Intelligence is in the bosom of every Soul, whether sinful or virtuous, waiting with infinite patience for it to wake up in meditation and be redeemed through Him.

The person who believes in this Christ Intelligence Saviour is not tortured by error, but the person who laughs at this thought is condemned to remain steeped in ignorance and to suffer until he wakes up. Unbelievers remain body-bound, and do not desire to seek the only path of salvation, through the Christ Intelligence.

Bask, therefore, in the true peace of the Universal Consciousness and let us remember our oneness with God. When, in life, we have so purged our personalities, our habits, our thinking, we have 20-20 vision with the Universal Consciousness. The promise is that we will all eventually awaken and feel like shouting, "Where have I been? What was I thinking?" Let the Second Coming of Christ unfold within us as we remember our oneness of body, mind, and spirit; our oneness with our brothers and sisters; and with the Creator.

ALL YOU NEED IS LOVE

After the tournaments, each knight galloped in the direction of his fancy. Rivalen rode up to King Mark's sister, bowed, and said, "God bless you, lovely lady."

Blanchefleur answered, "And may God who gladdens all hearts gladden yours. But you have hurt a friend of mine, the best I've ever had." Rivalen imagined that he had unwittingly injured a kinsperson of hers in the past. But no, the friend she was referring to was her heart.

This elegant depiction of the heart as our "best friend" is from Diane Wolkstein's beautiful rendering of the ancient story of Tristan and Iseult in her book, *The First Love Stories*. In it she re-tells the greatest stories of longing the world has known, ranging from Osiris and Isis to Eros and Psyche, from the Song of Songs to Shiva and Shakti. The stories of deep longing, superhuman devotion, impossible conflict, and miraculous transformation are "mysteries," writes the author. "Rooted in creation, separation, and rebirth . . . "

These ancient stories are analogies of the human heart, which endlessly seeks love through union with the partner; desiring to be rejoined with the soul mate, that other half of self with which we were one, in the beginning. Through marriages, friendships, love affairs, whatever form love, or our concept of it, takes, it is rare that a union of partners fills every void for very long in that "best friend" we've ever had, the heart. It's this "best friend" where the golden thread of oneness leads us next—to the secret place within where Universal Conciousness awaits us.

We actually seek oneness with God in every embrace, every union, every smile, every kindness, in every relationship. But our scriptures say that finding someone to love us according to our specific expectations won't bring us to oneness with God. If God is love, then giving love to others is ending separation and rejoining *oneness itself.* Giving will attract the love we desire.

A new commandment I give to you, that you love one another; even as I have loved you, that you also love one another. By this all men will know that you are my disciples, if you have love for one another. (John 13:34-35)

In 1924, Edgar Cayce was asked to define the law of love. Even though the answer is somewhat lengthy, it is provided below. Its importance goes far beyond a reminder of the golden rule or burdening our lives with yet one more law to obey. The fact is, the law of love is a universal law, as immutable as gravity, as much a law of physics as of morality.

(Q) What is the law of love?

(A) Giving. As is given in this injunction, "Love Thy Neighbor as Thyself." As is given in the injunction, "Love the Lord Thy God with all Thine Heart, Thine Soul and Thine Body." In this, as in many, we see upon the physical or earth or material plane the manifestations of that law, without the law itself. With any condition we find as this, which is the manifestation of the opposite from law of love. The gift, the giving, with hope of reward or pay is direct opposition of the law of love. Remember there is no greater than the injunction, "God so loved His Creation, or the World, as to give His Only Begotten Son, for their redemption." Through that love, as man makes it manifest in his own heart and life, does it reach that law, and in compliance of *a* Law, the law becomes a part of the individual. *That is the law of love.*

Giving in action, without the force felt, expressed, manifested, shown, desired or reward for that given. (3744-5)

Cayce had much to say about the importance of *giving love in action*—making oneness manifest through demonstration. It is the key to dissolving our separation from God—because separation from God is separation from love itself. This separation is the very root of our emptiness and our desire to find people who will give us love. Understanding the simple idea of giving love is the key to reawakening us to our oneness, to knowing I AM THAT I AM in the full promise that the Kingdom of Heaven lies within; where Universal Consciousness urges us onward in the center of our being.

In the same reading, Cayce adds to our understanding of this powerful key:

So we have *Love* is *Law, Law is Love. God is Love. Love is God.* In that we see the law manifested, not the law itself. Unto the individual, as we have given then, that gets the understanding of self, becomes a part of this. As is found, which come in one, so we have manifestations of the one-ness, of the all-ness in love. Now, if we, as individuals, upon the earth plane, have all of the other elementary forces that make to the bettering of life, and have not love we are as nothing—nothing. (3744-5)

The jewel of the concept of "love in action" is expressed in another reading that leads us along the golden thread to the center of our hearts—while looking for God in the "best friend" you've ever had, look for God in the "best friend" of another—the heart where Christ dwells, waiting to be drawn out through you in love demonstrated in action.

Yet know, until an individual entity—in time or space, or in acquaintanceship or in the friendship of an individual—*sees in every other entity* that he would worship in his Maker, he has not begun to have the proper concept of universal consciousness. (1747-5) [italics added]

Mouthing the words without demonstrating selfless love invites the caution Jesus gave when He said, "Not every one who says to me, 'Lord, Lord,' shall enter the kingdom of heaven, but he who does the will of my Father who is in heaven." (Matthew 7:21) The conscious decision to change the way we think and act takes time and effort. Carl Jung once said that "there is no birth of consciousness without pain." The Cayce readings advise that we apply ourselves diligently, once we decide to find our way to love's core—oneness:

Remember, there is no shortcut in becoming conscious of the God-force, which is a part of thine consciousness ... Life is lived within self. Ye live it; ye don't profess it ... (5392-1)

Knowledge of oneness cannot be realized by the simple desire to know. Neither can we expect results without applying spiritual truth through the hard work of resisting anything which separates us from oneness. The work is about you and me striving alone and together to know oneness again—it's just behind the thin curtain of our stubbornness and disbelief, just on the other side of love, where our "best friend" resides.

SERVICE WITH A SMILE

It is unfortunate that most Westerners have only one word for "love." The word is used to describe a thousand different acts and feelings, many of which have little to do with love as our Creator expresses it. Our word "love" can be too abstract when it comes down to putting "love" into action. Another word can help us, however, and that word is "service." We can more easily refocus our energies toward oneness and the Universal Consciousness by committing ourselves to some form of "service" to others.

In the lives of Buddha and Christ, we can find ample evidence of the miraculous power of love in action—service to others as a way of manifesting oneness with God. While on his death bed and wracked with pain, the aged Buddha commented with a smile that he could only remember two meals in his entire life. As a young man trying to discover true freedom from selfish desires, he nearly starved himself to death. He was saved, however, by a young girl who found him and brought him a simple meal. The meal that saved his life, therefore, was the first meal he remembered. The second meal that he remembered was a dish at a gathering that he insisted be given only to himself. This meal poisoned him and was the cause of his death.

The Buddha's search to rid the world of suffering brought him to the realization that the objects and fantasies of the world are only temporary and cannot sustain happiness. He cleaned out his mind and feelings, and even dodged the hungers of his body in order to find perfect compassion, and this is how he achieved Enlightenment. He had rejected wealth and pleasure, trading them for compassion and service. In Nirvana, the Buddha became one with the Ultimate Reality, through the Universal Consciousness of love and *service in action.*

Jesus' message of compassion pervades the New Testament. The Kingdom of Heaven, He shows, will be known through service, humility, and love. As Christ, Jesus was fully realized as one with the Father and one with the Universal Consciousness. He performed miraculous acts of compassion and healing throughout His life. He wept upon learning of the death of Lazarus. He wept over Jerusalem's fate and wept as He created food for the multitudes, simply because they were hungry. Jesus, too, shunned possessions and wealth, though it had all been offered to Him. He traveled and taught as Buddha had, 500 years before.

In keeping the ways open for a greater service, the joys of the service lighten the burdens of life. See in those thou meetest day by day the image that is as the spiritual light in *every* life. For, as the light of His love shines through thine own life, it may guide many a weary soul to a knowledge, an understanding of His love that is shed abroad in a weak and sin-weary world! (473-1)

Service is putting love into action in the world. It operates with the Law of Love as a godly act—the will of I AM THAT I AM being one with our will. Out of compassion, Buddha found the way to end suffering. Out of compassion, Christ, the Firstborn, preserved and restored the perfect pattern for us to follow back to our Creator.

Cayce actually defined the Universal Consciousness as service, when he said " . . . the universal awareness, the desire to be more of a universal help, without making a show—or less and less of self, and more and more of that influence which brought to the mind of the man Jesus the Christ Consciousness, the awareness of being at one with Him." (2282-1)

I AM THAT I AM stands at the ready, when we take our first steps inward to find oneness and first stretch our arms outward in service to others:

. . . it is ever those that draw nearer to the Universal Consciousness of the Christ that come closer to the perfect relationship to the Creative Forces or God, the Father—which the man Jesus attained when He gave of Himself to the world, that through Him, by and in Him, each entity might come to know the true relationship with the Father. (3357-2)

Let us dine together at the banquet of the Creator, and discover together how to experience oneness through Universal Consciousness—the way we were, in the beginning:

For, ye have been *chosen* from the foundations of the world for a service to thy fellow man, in and through Him that *made* the world. Be faithful, then. Be not unmindful of that thou may bring to pass—the *glory* of the Christ in the lives of those that are seeking—seeking! (281-22)

Universal Consciousness and our oneness with God have always been the fuel of the living flame of being. Every breath and heartbeat, every thought, sensation, and emotion have bloomed into existence through the mind, from the eternal atom of our consciousness, which we have shared with Christ since the creation of our souls:

Thus as He declares, "Behold I stand continuously before the door of thy consciousness, of thine own mansion. For thy body is indeed the temple of the living God." And there He has promised to meet thee. There ye make ready. There ye entertain. There ye meditate upon those influences, those choices ye make day by day. (2879-1)

One of the most valuable components of the Edgar Cayce readings is the *Search for God* study group course that was put together during the 1930s by a dedicated group of people who asked Cayce to help them live a spiritual life. The course contains an entire chapter on oneness, and the following paragraph describes the ideal attitude for service:

"We should never allow ourselves to feel separate and apart from God or our fellow man; for what affects our neighbor on the other side of the world affects us. The people of the earth are one great family. We should love without distinction, knowing that God is in all. By making ourselves perfect channels that His grace, mercy, peace, and love may flow through us, we come to realize more and more the Oneness of all creation." *(A Search for God, Book I,* Chapter 11, "The Lord Thy God Is One.")

THE CYCLE OF ONENESS

The purpose of this book has been to trace the golden thread of oneness from our present consciousness back to the moment of creation and then forward again in order to discover that oneness, though obscured through our habit of separation, has been within us all along. Further, it has provided a simple meditation practice by which we can contact Universal Consciousness and allow our soul's memory of oneness to become a powerful force for living a happier life. We have followed the golden thread through the common heart of the world's religions, back through the oneness teachings of Jesus, on back to Moses and the holy name of oneness, I AM THAT I AM. Further still, we followed it back to Joseph, Jacob, and Abraham, and their sojourns in Egypt.

We then traced the powerful message of oneness through the ancient Egypt of recorded history and beyond, into the psychic records of an older Egypt and its role in preserving the I AM THAT I AM name from the Atlantean Law of One. We journeyed on back to Lemuria, to the time when we began to fashion forms and consciously chose to separate from oneness. The golden thread then led us to our divine origin, the pure state of our blissful existence in the eternity of the Universal Consciousness—when we spun out like blissful sparks from God's ecstatic creation of sentient companions.

But then, we looked for a divine solution for our loss of Universal Consciousness and our separation from oneness, and discovered the Creator's plan to bring us back. We followed the steps of the Firstborn, Amilius, the Master Soul, in His plan to unite us once again with God, with uniform bodies and the spiritual tools we'd need to use our free will correctly. We traced His own errors, difficult choices, and His hard work as Adam, Enoch, Melchizedek, and Hermes, when he and Ra Ta preserved the Law of One in the Hall of Records.

We followed the golden thread of oneness which the Firstborn carried forth with the help of "the sons of the Most High," laying the foundation for the birth and training of Jesus. Finally, we returned to our own day and the time of the Second Coming, and followed the golden thread of oneness to its home—within the heart, the "best friend" we have had, our holy Christ Self, since the beginning.

The suggestions for meditation given in chapter 6 are tried and true and can help you keep yourself aligned with your determination to "know thyself" as part of oneness. Aspire to access the Universal Consciousness by making God a part of manifest reality in the world through love and service, and don't forget to ask God for help, through grace, along the way. We finally discovered that the path to oneness is in service to others. In service, shall we all experience our memory of oneness:

For, with that power of will are we the sons of God—capable of being equal *with* Him in the glory that He would share with us. As He gave, "I and the Father are One, and ye in me, I in the Father—" These, then, should aid all in making that contribution that enables all to *want*, to *desire*, to be on fire with that desire, to *manifest* the Oneness of the Father in Life. For, as He is Life—we in Life may make manifest that our desires, our hearts, our minds, our souls, are *one* with Him in bringing to the knowledge of one—*anyone*—*everyone*—that the power of God, through the Christ, is able to save; even unto the utmost. (262-42)

Let us each display our best inner beauty, share the talents of our individuality, and dedicate the uniqueness of our love for God. In this we can know, even now, that we are one.

EXERCISES FOR LIVING ONENESS

In *Experiments in a Search for God*, a companion volume to *A Search for God, Book I*, Mark Thurston, Ph.D., offers the following exercise that can be of great help in our search for oneness.

Experiment #1:   Examine your life and choose one way in which you are using energy which is not in accord with your ideals. This can be an emotional, attitudinal, or active way of using energy. Write down what you select. Then demonstrate in your daily life your understanding of the inherent oneness of all force by transforming that energy to a more loving or constructive form. Record your experiences.

Example: Feeling frustrated and angry with automobile drivers who are discourteous.

Transformation: Changing your expression of the one energy, by sending out to those travelers a prayer, instead of thoughts of anger.

Experiment #2:   In your relationship with others live with an attitude that the body, mind, and soul are one. Especially work to apply the understanding that the way in which you treat the body (yours or someone else's) is the way you are treating the soul.

Experiment #3:   In your daily contacts with others, imagine that they are part of your immediate family. If you feel apathetic or upset with someone, try to imagine how you might feel more caring or tolerant if that person were a close and beloved family member. Then try to act on that new feeling. Record instances in which you try this experiment, the family member status you imagine for him or her, and how you acted on the feeling.

Example:

person:	a stranger I was sitting next to on the bus
family status imagined:	that she was my sister
action:	I struck up a friendly conversation with her instead of just sitting silently next to her.

(The above material is used by permission of A.R.E. Press. The exercises can be found in *Experiments in a Search for God*, Mark A. Thurston, Ph.D., on pages 119 to 128.)

Selected Reading List

Agee, Doris. *Edgar Cayce on ESP.* New York: Warner Books, 1969.

Angus, S. *The Mystery-Religions: A Study in the Religious Background of Early Christianity.* New York: Dover Publications, Inc., 1975.

Bauval, Robert, and Gilbert, Adrian. *The Orion Mystery.* New York: Crown Trade Paperbacks, 1996.

Bercholz, Samuel, and Kohn, Sher Ab Chödzin (eds.). *Entering the Stream: An Introduction to the Buddha and His Teachings.* Boston: Shambhala Publications, Inc., 1993.

Budge, E. A. Wallis. *The Book of the Dead.* New York: Bell Publishing Co., 1960.

_____ *The Book of the Dead.* New York: Dover Publications, Inc., 1967.

Callahan, Kathy L. *Our Origin and Destiny: An Evolutionary Perspective on the New Millennium.* Virginia Beach, Virginia: A.R.E. Press, 1996.

Cayce, Edgar Evans. *Edgar Cayce on Atlantis.* New York: Warner Books, 1968.

Cayce, Edgar Evans, Schwartzer, Gail Cayce, and Richards, Douglas G. *Mysteries of Atlantis Revisited.* New York: St. Martins Press, Inc., 1996.

Cayce, Hugh Lynn. *Venture Inward.* Virginia Beach, Virginia: A.R.E. Press, 1996.

Cervé, W. S. *Lemuria: The Lost Continent of the Pacific.* (Volume XII of the Rosicrucian Library Series.) San Jose, California: The Rosicrucian Press, Ltd., 1982.

Chambers, John D. (trans.). *The Divine Pymander and Other Writings of Hermes Trismegistus.* New York: Samuel Weiser, Inc., 1975.

Church, W.H. *The Lives of Edgar Cayce.* Virginia Beach, Virginia: A.R.E. Press, 1996.

Churchward, James. *The Lost Continent of Mu.* New York: Ives Washburn, Publisher, 1933.

Daniélou, Alain. *The Myths and Gods of India.* Rochester, Vermont: Inner Traditions International, Ltd., 1991.

De Camp, L. Sprague. *Lost Continents: The Atlantis Theme in History, Science, and Literature.* New York: Dover Publications, Inc., 1970.

Donath, Dorothy C. *Buddhism for the West: Theravada, Mahayana, Vajrayana.* New York: Julian Press, Inc., 1971.

Donnelly, I. *Atlantis: The Antediluvian World.* (Revised by Egerton Sykes.) New York: Harper & Brothers, 1949.

Douglas-Klotz, Neil. *Desert Wisdom: Sacred Middle Eastern Writings from the Goddess Through the Sufis.* San Francisco: HarperSanFrancisco, 1995.

Earll, Tony. *Mu Revealed.* New York: Coronet Communications, Inc., 1970.

Feuerstein, Georg. *Encyclopedic Dictionary of Yoga.* New York: Paragon House, 1990.

Frawley, David. *Gods, Sages, and Kings: Vedic Secrets of Ancient Civilizations.* Salt Lake City, Utah: Passage Press, 1991.

Gaskell, G. A. *Dictionary of All Scriptures and Myths.* New York: Gramercy Books, 1981.

Goldsmith, Joel S. *Consciousness Unfolding.* New York: University Books, Inc., 1962.

Hahn, Thich Nhat. *The Miracle of Mindfulness.* Boston: Beacon Press, 1976.

Hancock, Graham. *Fingerprints of the Gods: The Evidence of Earth's Lost Civilization.* New York: Crown Publishers, Inc., 1995.

Hancock, Graham, and Bauval, Robert. *The Message of the Sphinx: A Quest for the Hidden Legacy of Mankind.* New York: Crown Publishers, Inc., 1996.

Krajenke, Robert W. *From the Birth of Souls to the Death of Moses.* Virginia Beach, Virginia: A.R.E. Press, 1992.

_____ *From Joshua to the Golden Age of Solomon.* Virginia Beach, Virginia: A.R.E. Press, 1992.

_____ *From Solomon's Glories to the Birth of Jesus.* Virginia Beach, Virginia: A.R.E. Press, 1992.

_____ *Spiritual Power Points: A Guide to Hidden Oases Along the Spiritual Path.* Virginia Beach, Virginia: A.R.E. Press, 1997.

Landone, Brown. *Prophecies of Melchi-Zedek in the Great Pyramid and the Seven Temples.* New York: The Book of Gold, 1940.

LaViolette, Paul A. *Beyond the Big Bang: Ancient Myth and the Science of Continuous Creation.* Rochester, Vermont: Park Street Press, 1995.

Lehner, Mark. *Our Egyptian Heritage.* Virginia Beach, Virginia: A.R.E. Press, 1974.

Lemkow, Anna F. *The Wholeness Principle: Dynamics of Unity Within Science, Religion, and Society.* Wheaton, Illinois: The Theosophical Publishing House, 1990.

LeShan, Lawrence. *The Medium, the Mystic, and the Physicist: Toward a General Theory of the Paranormal.* New York: Penguin Books USA, Inc., 1974.

Lodrö, Geshe Gedün. *Walking Through Walls: A Presentation of Tibetan Meditation.* Ithaca, New York: Snow Lion Publications, 1992.

Mitchell, Stephen. *Genesis: A New Translation of the Classic Biblical Stories.* New York: HarperCollins, 1996.

Naydler, Jeremy. *Temple of the Cosmos: The Ancient Egyptian Experience of the Sacred.* Rochester, Vermont: Inner Traditions International, 1996.

Nelson, Kirk. *The Second Coming.* Virginia Beach, Virginia: Wright Publishing Company, 1992.

Nigosian, Solomon. *Judaism: The Way of Holiness.* London: The Aquarian Press, 1987.

Pagels, Elaine. *The Gnostic Gospels.* New York: Vintage Books, 1981.

Plato. *The Works of Plato: Four Volumes in One.* New York: Tudor Publishing Co. (no year).

Powers, John. *Introduction to Tibetan Buddhism.* Ithaca, New York: Snow Lion Publications, 1995.

Puryear, Herbert B. *The Edgar Cayce Primer: Discovering the Path to Self-Transformation.* New York: Bantam Books, 1982.

Puryear, Herbert B., and Thurston, Mark A. *Meditation and the Mind of Man.* Virginia Beach, Virginia: A.R.E. Press, 1988.

Redford, Donald B. *Akhenaten: The Heretic King.* Princeton, New Jersey: Princeton University Press, 1987.

Reed, Henry. *Your Mind: Unlocking Your Hidden Powers.* Virginia Beach, Virginia: A.R.E. Press, 1996.

Rinpoche, Kalu. *The Gem Ornament of Manifold Oral Instructions.* Ithaca, New York: Snow Lion Publications, 1991.

Robinson, James M. (gen. ed.). *The Nag Hammadi Library.* New York: HarperCollins Publishers, 1988.

Robinson, Lytle. *Edgar Cayce's Story of the Origin and Destiny of Man.* New York: The Berkley Publishing Group, 1976.

Sanderfur, Glenn. *Lives of the Master.* Virginia Beach, Virginia: A.R.E. Press, 1988.

Satchidananda, S. Swami. *The Golden Present.* Buckingham, Virginia: Integral Publications, 1987.

_____ (trans.). *The Yoga Sutras of Patanjali.* Buckingham, Virginia: Integral Yoga Publications, 1990.

Schaya, Leo. *The Universal Meaning of the Kabbalah.* Secaucus, New Jersey: University Books, Inc., 1971.

Scholem, Gershom G. *On the Kabbalah and Its Symbolism.* (Translated by Ralph Manheim.) New York: Schocken Books, 1965.

Scott, Walter. *Hermetica.* Boulder, Colorado: Hermes House, 1982.

Search for God, A, Book I. Virginia Beach, Virginia: A.R.E. Press, 1986.

Sharp, Daryl. *Jung Lexicon: A Primer of Terms and Concepts.* Toronto: Inner City Books, 1991.

Smith, A. Robert. "The Sphinx: Older by Half?" *Venture Inward* (January/February 1992): 14.

Smith, Huston. *The Religions of Man.* New York: Harper & Row, Publishers, Inc., 1958.

Sparrow, Lynn Elwell. *Reincarnation—Claiming Your Past, Creating Your Future.* New York: Harper & Row, Publishers, Inc., 1988.

Spence, Lewis. *The History of Atlantis.* New York: Bell Publishing Company, 1968.

Sproul, Barbara C. *Primal Myths: Creating the World.* New York: Harper & Row, Publishers, Inc., 1979.

Stewart, R.J. *The Elements of Creation Myth.* Longmead, Shaftsbury, Dorset: Element Books Ltd., 1989.

Stone, Merlin. *When God Was a Woman*. New York: Harcourt Brace & Company, 1976.

Sugrue, Thomas. *There Is a River*. Virginia Beach, Virginia: A.R.E. Press, 1971.

Tanner, Florice. *The Mystery Teachings in World Religions*. Wheaton, Illinois: The Theological Publishing House, 1973.

Thurston, Mark A. *Experiments in a Search for God*. Virginia Beach, Virginia: A.R.E. Press, 1976.

Thurston, Mark A., and Fazel, Christopher. *The Edgar Cayce Handbook for Creating Your Future*. New York: Ballantine Books, 1992.

Trungpa, Chögyam. *The Myth of Freedom and the Way of Meditation*. Berkeley & London: Shambhala Publications, 1976.

Van Auken, John. *Spiritual Breakthrough*. Virginia Beach, Virginia: A.R.E. Press, 1996.

Walters, J. Donald. *Superconsciousness: A Guide to Meditation*. New York: Warner Books, 1996.

Weatherhead, Leslie D. *The Christian Agnostic*. Nashville, Tennessee: Abingdon Press, 1965.

Whitman, Walt. *Complete Prose Works: Democratic Vistas*. Philadelphia: David McKay, 1892.

Wilson, Louis F. *A Universal Pattern of Consciousness*. Hanover, Massachusetts: The Christopher Publishing House, 1994.

Wise, Michael, Agegg, Martin, Jr., and Cook, Edward. *The Dead Sea Scrolls: A New Translation*. San Francisco: HarperSanFransisco, 1996.

Wolkstein, Diane. *The First Love Stories: From Isis and Osiris to Tristan and Iseult*. New York: HarperCollins, 1991.

Yeshe, Lama. *Introduction to Tantra: A Vision of Totality*. Boston: Wisdom Publications, 1987.

Yogananda, Paramahansa. *The Second Coming of Christ*. Dallas, Texas: Amitra Foundation, Inc., 1979.

You Can Receive Books Like This One
and Much, Much More

You can begin to receive books in the *A.R.E. Membership Series* and many more benefits by joining the nonprofit Association for Research and Enlightenment, Inc., as a Sponsoring or Life member.

The A.R.E. has a worldwide membership that receives a wide variety of study aids, all aimed at assisting individuals in their spiritual, mental, and physical growth.

Every member of A.R.E. receives a copy of *Venture Inward*, the organization's bimonthly magazine; an in-depth journal, *The New Millennium* on alternate months; opportunity to borrow, through the mail, from a collection of more than 500 files on medical and metaphysical subjects; access to one of the world's most complete libraries on metaphysical and spiritual subjects; and opportunities to participate in conferences, international tours, a retreat-camp for children and adults, and numerous nationwide volunteer activities.

In addition to the foregoing benefits, Sponsoring and Life members also receive at no charge three books each year in the *A.R.E. Membership Series*.

If you are interested in finding out more about membership in A.R.E. and the many benefits that can assist you on your path to fulfillment, you can easily contact the Membership Department by writing Membership, A.R.E., P.O. Box 595, Virginia Beach, VA 23451-0595 or by calling **1-800-333-4499** or faxing **1-757-422-6921**.

Explore our electronic visitor's center on the Internet:
http://www.are-cayce.com

CONTENTS